/03

JOHN DEERE
SMALL TRACTORS

Rod Beemer

MBI Publishing Company

To everyone who has hand-cranked a two-lunger on a snowy, subzero winter morning or under the blazing sun on a 110-degree summer afternoon.

First published in 2002 by MBI Publishing Company, Galtier Plaza, Suite 200, 380 Jackson Street, St. Paul, MN 55101-3885 USA

MBI Publishing Company books are also available at discounts in bulk quantity for industrial or sales-promotional use. For details write to Special Sales Manager at Motorbooks International Wholesalers & Distributors, Galtier Plaza, Suite 200, 380 Jackson Street, St. Paul, MN 55101-3885 USA.

Library of Congress Cataloging-in-Publication Data
0-7603-1130-7

Author Bio: Rod Beemer is a custom furniture designer and builder and an experienced writer who has written numerous books, including *John Deere: A Factory History* and *John Deere New Generation Tractors*. He lives in Bennington, Kansas, with his wife, Dawn.

On the front cover: A 1956 Model 320 Utility made an excellent agricultural haying tractor or a great mowing vehicle for maintaining highway right-of-ways. At a 1958 price of $1,885, it was an economical way to do both.

Frontispiece: The downward-directed exhaust is another feature that helps identify an orchard model. In this case, it's a 1936 BO. A total of 5,083 copies of the BO were manufactured.

On the title page: A welcome feature of John Deere's two-cylinder design was simplicity, at a time when farmers had to learn the new skills required to maintain and repair tractors. Farmers often relied on the local blacksmith to keep horsepower, like this team of Belgian horses and a 1941 Model LA, operating smoothly.

On the back cover: *Top* It stands only 52 1/2 inches high, with shields over the air intake and fuel tank caps. It must be a BO—a 1936 brass tag, first-year production BO on full steel. *Bottom* This Model 430 Hi-Crop just begs to be photographed.

Edited by Chad Caruthers
Designed by Katie Sonmor

Printed in Hong Kong

CONTENTS

ACKNOWLEDGMENTS

There's a wealth of information in the Deere & Company archives in Moline, Illinois, as well as magazine after magazine and book after book, on John Deere tractors. Each is a valuable resource.

However, Deere personnel, past and present, are equally valuable resources, for they are the individuals who birthed the enduring and legendary John Deere machines. They are the engineers who, with a slide rule, a mathematical formula, and boundless creativity, rendered a concept into a blueprint. They are the factory workers who, with these blueprints, cast the iron and steel and machined the components that ultimately emerged at the end of the assembly line as a John Deere tractor.

I thank the following retired Deere employees, who have given me a wealth of time, information, and courtesy: Mike Mack, director, Product Engineering Center; Fred Hileman, director of service, Marketing Division; and Warren Wiele, Robert Guetzlaff, and Danny Gleeson, engineers.

Other great resources include the collectors and restorers who rescue and revitalize these artifacts of our agricultural heritage. I thank these individuals, especially those who have spent innumerable hours polishing up and rolling out their tractors for my camera: Mel Kopf; John Nikodym; Kenny, Harland, and Lester Layher; Joe Roy; Larry Dennis; Bob Lee; Charles Dugan; Leo Zeigler; Darrell M. Hills; Earl and Harold Hartzog; Don and Donna Nolde; Don J. Klaus; Andy and Karen Anderson; and Mark F. Strasser.

Thanks also to Norris Maydew for hitching up and posing his team of Belgian horses; to blacksmiths Larry Neilson and Steve Plenert, who added a bit of authenticity and nostalgia to this tractor-versus-horse story; and to Brent Sampson, test engineer, Nebraska Tractor Test Laboratory, who fielded many questions.

Finally, thanks to anyone and everyone whom I may have overlooked.

INTRODUCTION

At the dawn of the tractor era, Deere & Company's position seemed to be, "What should we do with this idea of tractors?" Then, the perspective became, "How can we *do* this idea of tractors?" Of course, it didn't take Deere long to answer these questions, and over the following decades the company seemed to solve problems before they existed and create answers before there were questions. It's the stuff that legends are made of, and Deere did this better than any other tractor company.

At the start of twentieth century, the Industrial Revolution was changing life not only in urban America but in rural America, as well. John Deere had improved, and in fact transformed, the plow; Cyrus McCormick had successfully revolutionized harvesting; and J. I. Case had mechanized the labor-intensive job of threshing.

Another revolutionary development, steam power, was beginning to replace equine and bovine muscle to draw the plow, pull the reaper, and power the thresher. But it would take several decades and the internal combustion engine to finally put the nation's millions of work horses and mules out to pasture.

After all, there was a certain comfort and continuity about horse horsepower. A horse was a horse was a horse. Some were bigger and stronger than others, and generation after generation of farmers grew up understanding work animals—how they worked, how to raise them, and how to get the most out of them. And, while selective breeding made it possible to improve the horse, and upgraded implements such as the improved steel plow helped, for generations the general rule of thumb remained, "You can plow an acre per horse per day." At the time, no one ever dreamed of a single "horse" that could be bred to do the work of 30, 50, or even 100 horses.

When tractors began popping up on farms, however, they were a very different animal indeed. For the builders of those very first tractors, such as the 1892 Froelich and the 1894 Otto, there were no blueprints to follow. Whether they were engineers, CEOs, designers, or builders, they carved the fuel, ignition, transmission, and structural design out of trial and error. Nobody knew for sure what a tractor should look like, what exactly it should do, or how it should work.

Despite the numerous early imperfections, there were visionaries who saw through the complications and realized the enormous potential of the gasoline-powered traction engine. For farmers, tractors represented the Industrial Revolution brought home, offering hope for improved efficiency and relief from the grinding physical labor required to put bread on the table. Entrepreneurs saw the embryonic tractor as a potential for enormous profits and wondered if only a machine could be perfected to replace the horses and mules on even the very smallest of farms. They measured this potential market in millions of sales and dollars.

ABOUT THIS BOOK

This is the history of the evolution of John Deere's small two-cylinder tractors—mechanical muscle designed for small-acreage operations and intended for the farmer who couldn't afford a 15-ton behemoth yet wanted to do his work easier and quicker via tractor power.

While focused on John Deere, this book also takes a look at other companies' small tractors to help illustrate the intense focus that the industry had on eliminating horses and mules from small farms. By including information on the evolution of *tractors*, and not just John Deere, it is easier to see the many engineering advances that occurred across the board during this period.

The primary focus of this book, however, is John Deere. This is the story of how Deere & Company's small, general-purpose tractors helped make obsolete the very horse-drawn equipment that built John Deere's company.

Chapter 1

SIX- TO EIGHT- HORSE TRACTORS

Models C, GP, GPWT, P, and B

Deere & Company moved cautiously into the tractor era, as indicated in a 1918 company bulletin in which a Deere manager cautioned salesmen about overselling the Waterloo Boy tractor by reminding them that, "The foundation of the John Deere business is building agricultural implements for use with horses." The manager further warned that, "Least of all should we conclude that the horse will be ultimately eliminated." In conclusion, he expressed the company's belief that the horse would continue to be the main power source for farm work.

Atricycle front axle, over-the-hood steering, and an exposed flywheel established the look of unstyled row-crop John Deere tractors for many years. The Unstyled G, A, and B all bear a strong family resemblance.

Today this view may seem extremely shortsighted or overly cautious. But at that time, the workhorse and working mule population reached its peak, which, according to the U.S. Census, was 21 million horses and more than 5 million mules.

If its initial move toward power farming was cautious, it was also certain. History shows that Deere & Company quickly recognized the ultimate fate of the horse and mule by responding to the increasing demands for tractor power in agriculture. Deere established a respectable presence in the tractor market with the famous Model D of 1924. In 1928, Deere introduced its first row-crop tractor, which would retire many horse and mule teams from even the smallest farms. That same year, the horse and mule population had dropped to just over 19 million head, down some 7 million, as the impact of small gasoline tractors increased.

At present the leading manufacturer of agricultural equipment goods and services, Deere & Company has not only survived, but remains as the only major long-line U.S. agricultural manufacturing company that has never been sold or merged with another company. Its operations circumvent the globe. Certainly, from horses to horsepower, Deere has come a long way.

MODEL C: 1927–1928

Developmental work on John Deere's All-Crop tractor began in 1925. Like the Farmall, John Deere's All-Crop was aimed at doing numerous farm jobs, in particular, planting and cultivating row crop.

In early 1927, the All-Crop name was changed to the Model C, and production began in March 1928. By April, about 100 tractors bore the Model C designation, but at least 53 of these were recalled by the company and ultimately

This rare Model C, serial number 200201, was built on April 20, 1928. Out of a production run of 100 copies, it was one of the last 10 Model Cs built. At least half of these were recalled by the company, rebuilt, and then tagged as Model GPs.

rebuilt and renumbered as Model GPs. Only a handful of original Model Cs are known to exist, which perhaps leaves a few yet to be discovered by hopeful collectors.

The Model C was very similar in design to the Model D but on a smaller scale. The Model D, which proved to be a great success for both farmer and Deere & Company, was first and foremost a drawbar tractor designed as the power source for pull-type implements. Although some effort was made to adapt the Model D to row-crop work, the Model C was the first big step toward Deere fielding a successful row-crop tractor.

The proven design of the Waterloo Boy's horizontal two-cylinder engine was continued in the Model D and also in the Model C. The Model C's flathead engine was a 5-3/4x6-inch bore and stroke, which displaced 312 ci. It was rated at 950 rpm, and produced 17 drawbar and 24 belt horsepower. It was a kerosene burner with water injection into the carburetor to help minimize detonation under heavy load. A 3/1 transmission provided 2-1/4, 3, and 4 mile per-hour forward speeds and 1-3/4 mile per hour reverse speeds.

Operator comfort obviously wasn't a priority when the Model C's seat was designed. It would be another two decades before Deere's tractor seats were operator friendly. However, the wood steering wheel adds a real touch of class.

This close-up of the brass carburetor on this Model C, serial number 200201, shows the water-feed line and control link. Water was drawn from the radiator and fed into the cylinder to control detonation.

In addition to the serial number, this brass ID plate gives the Model C's horsepower as 10–20 and the rpm as 950. These are Deere & Company's test results, as the Model C was never tested at Nebraska.

Several design features are vintage Model C, such as a vertical seat support; rear-wheel hubs that are flat, or level; an exhaust end that is cut straight across; wooden steering wheel; brass carburetor with water-feed valve; and priming-cup housings on the rear axle. These features helped the Model C stand a little taller to accommodate row-crop work. Experimental versions of the Model C were produced with a tricycle front axle and coupled with two- and four-row implements. However, the standard model was a three-row outfit. The Model C was not tested at Nebraska.

MODEL GP (GENERAL PURPOSE) STANDARD: 1928–1935

Engineering changes and a new model designation, namely, the Model GP Standard, were introduced in August 1928. The "GP" designation reflected the general-purpose role of the

In the foreground is a 1938 BR on full steel. It shares the corner of a private museum with the 1930 GP, shown in the background.

FORDSON
1917-1928

Henry Ford was obsessed with the prospect of replacing horse power with mechanical power, and with the Fordson he succeeded several million times over.

From the Fordson's introduction in 1917 until 1928, when U.S. production ended, approximately 750,000 tractors had rolled off Ford's Dearborn and Rouge assembly lines, replacing approximately three to six million workhorses in the United States.

The Fordson was primarily a drawbar-only power source, which in many cases hooked onto a pull-type implement that had only recently been drawn by a team of horses. Although later versions were targeted at row-crop farming, the Fordson wasn't a general purpose tractor around the farm.

One of the Fordson's noteworthy features was its innovative uniframe, one of the first in the tractor industry. Rather than a conventional frame, the Fordson had a cast-iron engine, transmission, and axle housing that served as the frame for the tractor.

A drawback of the Fordson was the tractor's proclivity to flip over backward when a trailing implement encountered an obstruction, such as a hidden tree stump. Specially designed fenders helped, but didn't entirely alleviate this problem.

The Model F was powered by a vertical four-cylinder engine with a 4x5-inch bore and stroke, which displaced 251-ci and was rated at 1,000 rpm. The engine ran on either gasoline or kerosene. The three-speed transmission offered forward working speeds of 1.3, 2.7, and 6.8 miles per hour forward and 2.6 in reverse. The wheelbase was 63 inches, and the vehicle weighed in at 2,710 pounds. The 1918 price of $750 was lowered to $395 in 1922, just as the "tractor wars" commenced.

After Ford discontinued U.S. production in 1928, Irish Fordsons were built at Cork, Ireland, until 1932, when production was moved to Dagenham, England. Here, the improved Model N was manufactured until 1945.

Nebraska Test 18: Fordson
Date: 1920 Fuel: Kerosene HP: 9 Drawbar, 19 Belt
Nebraska Test 124: Fordson
Date: 1926 Fuel: Kerosene HP: 12 Drawbar, 22 Belt

Far from any bean field, this Bean tractor awaits restoration in a John Deere nesting ground in Nebraska. It is recognizable as a Bean tractor by the extrawide front axle on a GP Standard.

tractor. The mechanical changes corrected problems that had surfaced in the Model C during its short lifetime.

The GP, an improved version of the Model C, sported a new-style seat support and "General Purpose" on top of the hood. The round exhaust pipe was cut at an angle, which gives the end an oval appearance.

GP Standard serial numbers begin in 1928 with 200211 and end in 1935 at number 230745. Seventy-three tricycle GPs were produced from 1928 to 1929, and today few complete tractors of this model are known to exist. Existing tricycle GPs carry GP Standard Tread serial numbers and were built prior to the GPWT.

The early GP's two-cylinder engine displaced 312-ci from a 5-3/4x6-inch bore and stroke rated at 950 rpm, which was the same as the Model C. Nebraska test number 153, conducted in 1928, recorded 17 drawbar and 24 belt horsepower. The

This 1932 GP Wide-Tread with over-the-hood steering is one of 443 copies manufactured. The serial numbers for the GPWT range from 404810 through 405254. The serial number for this tractor is 405060.

GP test tractor, serial number 200112, had the 312-ci engine and operated on kerosene.

Fred Hileman, who began working for Deere & Company in 1925 and retired in 1969 as director of service in the Marketing Division, remembered a problem they had with the GP near Corpus Christi, Texas. He was sent to discover the cause and provide a solution. "The original GP tractor had a water-feed valve that took water from the cooling system and introduced it at the carburetor. When the tractor was pulling hard, the engine would ping from cheap fuel, so the farmer would open that water-feed valve to kill that knock.

"Well, because of a problem with the water-feed valve, it was decided to eliminate it. Then the final drive gears were changed to prevent them from putting as much strain on the engine, which therefore eliminated the knock—and also

Tagged with serial number 209392, this 1929 Model GP sports a mounted John Deere mower with 7-foot sicklebar. Power was provided by the tractor's PTO, which eliminated the wheel slippage that often occurred with mowers pulled by horses or tractors.

Lots of clearance under the rear axle housings, wide tread, and 18 drawbar horsepower were some of the features that made the GP Wide-Tread capable of four-row planting and cultivation. This restored tractor is fitted with the optional rear fenders.

slowed the tractor down, though a farmer had no way of knowing how fast it was going.

"These changes were all done as a field conversion, and they became a production change. Not all tractors in the field got the conversion, so there are some tractors out there with the original gearing."

The original GP tractors proved underpowered for three-row cultivation, so in May 1930, the Crossover GP Standards, sometimes known as the X/O GPs, were introduced. From serial number 223803 and on, the bore was increased to 6 inches, while the stroke remained the same, resulting in a square engine that displaced 339-ci. The rated rpm remained 950, and this new, larger engine did not have the water injection system. Both the 315-ci and 339-ci engines were mated to a 3/1 transmission capable of 2-1/4, 3, and 4 miles per hour forward and 1-3/4 in reverse. The GP Standard Crossover tractors are a rare unit, as only some 68 were produced.

The GP was introduced as a standard (wide) front axle that was arched to straddle the center row of row

The Lindeman Company of Yakima, Washington, purchased a number of GPOs and fitted them with a crawler undercarriage. These orchard crawlers became known as the GPO-Lindemans. Only about 25 units were manufactured. This 1935 example carries serial number 0-15704.

MOLINE UNIVERSAL MODEL D
1917-1923

The Moline Plow Company of Moline, Illinois, had a direct, but small, link to Deere & Company and a large, notable claim to fame among early tractor manufacturers.

Henry W. Candee and Robert K. Swan formed Candee, Swan & Company in 1852 to build fanning mills that would clean grain. In 1865, the company decided to enter the plow manufacturing arena. Much of the know-how for this venture came from Andrew Friberg, a former Deere & Company employee who joined Candee and Swan as a partner.

In 1868, another partner joined the firm and the name was changed to the Moline Plow Company. The company was very successful. From 1895 to 1910, the volume of business doubled every five years, with gross sales for the year ending June 30, 1913, estimated at $15 million.

The company entered the "power farming" trend by purchasing the Universal Tractor Manufacturing Company of Columbus, Ohio. The Universal Tractor featured two large drive wheels located in front, and the engine sat between. In the rear, light-truck wheels supported the operator and implement. It had the appearance of a giant garden tractor—one that weighed 3,590 pounds! But at that point in time, farmers wanted tractor power on the farm, and soon the company experienced record sales.

The November 30, 1916, issue of *Farm Implements* lauded the operation as having the "Largest Tractor Plant in The World," stating that the Moline Plow Company's new plant in Rock Island, Illinois, covered 5-1/2 acres of floor space.

The improved four-cylinder Universal Model D was introduced in 1917, and by 1918 it featured an electric self-starter and electric headlights as standard equipment. The company-built overhead valve four-cylinder engine displaced 192-ci from a 3-1/2x5-inch bore and stroke rated at 1,800 rpm. This was one of the first farm tractors with a variable-speed governor.

The line of implements designed especially for the Universal Model D included a rear carrying truck, disc harrow, grain drill, planter, lister, cultivator, mower, grain binder, corn binder, and manure spreader.

The company offered an Orchard Model and an Industrial Model, called the Moline Road Tractor, before it ceased tractor production in 1923. Without any added weight, the Model D tipped the scales at 3,380 pounds. The base price in 1917 for the tractor only was $700, plus another $35 if the customer wanted the riding truck attachment.

Nebraska Test 33: Moline Universal Model D

Date: 1920   Fuel: Gasoline   HP: 17 Drawbar, 27 Belt

The air intake stack on this GPO-Lindeman doesn't protrude above the hood, and the exhaust is positioned horizontally. It is therefore well below the hood line, providing a low profile for working around and under trees.

crop when cultivating, which enabled it to work three rows. Mounted three-row cultivators and planters were available, along with an optional mechanical power lift and 540-rpm PTO. Individual rear-wheel brakes were standard equipment.

Several major changes occurred to the Model GP before it was discontinued in 1935. Initial models had the air intake system located behind the radiator, and the spark plugs were tilted upward to allow extra clearance. Late in 1929, the air intake stack was routed through the right side of the hood. Prior to this change, the stack ran up beside the hood on the tractor's right side.

With the Crossover models, the air intake stack was moved outside the hood on the left, and the exhaust was moved to the right side. Other changes included improvements to the radiator core, guard, and curtains, and improved crankcase breather and oil filter. The priming-cup compression-release cocks were discontinued and replaced with the standard compression-release design.

Several options were available, including rubber tires, an extrawide front axle, and a lighting package. All Model Cs and early GPs and GPWTs were of the side-steer design until 1932, when over-the-hood steering was introduced on the GPWT. The basic Model GP weighed in at approximately 4,100 pounds.

The price of the 1928 GP was about $850, while the GP Standard in 1935 listed for about $950. One source lists the GP as having a price tag of $800 in 1928 and another source lists the Standard GP on rubber going for $950 in 1933. Of course, one in fine condition today would bring in much more.

While the GP Standard certainly represents an important step in the evolution of the tractor, the three-row configuration and a lack of power made it a disappointment to both Deere and farmers of the day.

Nebraska Test 153: GP Standard
Date: 1928   Fuel: Kerosene   HP: 17 Drawbar, 24 Belt

This 1935 BN is also known as a B Garden, due to Deere's marketing material targeted at California's vegetable growers. With only 11 drawbar and 16 belt horsepower, it was ideal for vegetable farming.

This 1935 BN is 1 of only 24 built using the four-bolt pedestal. Experimental part numbers cast into the pedestal are clearly visible.

Bean Tractor

Another special application of the GP Standard was the Bean tractor, which was modified to fit the four-row requirements of edible-bean and beet growers. Bean tractors were fitted with an extended front axle. In addition, the offset-hub rear wheels were reversed and moved to opposite sides.

The optional parts necessary to convert a GP to a Bean tractor became available in 1931. In 1933, rubber tires were added as an additional option.

MODEL GP WIDE-TREAD: 1929–1933

In July 1929, the GP Wide-Tread (GPWT) went into production side by side with the GP Standard. Rear axles set at 84 inches coupled with a tricycle front axle gave Deere its first real contender in the row-crop tractor market. A departure from the unpopular three-row design, the GPWT could accommodate two- or four-row planting and cultivating implements.

Production of the GPWT ended in October 1933. The serial number range is 400000 to 405254. Like its sibling, the GP, the GPWT began life with the 5-3/4x6-inch bore and

tapered fuel tank and hood, which greatly improved operator visibility. To further aid the operator's ability to see while working row crop, the exhaust and air intake were positioned within the hood line. The air cleaner was actually mounted in the radiator's top tank, and the exhaust ran through the radiator's top tank.

Production was slowed during the depression years of 1932 and 1933, and only 443 of the final-version Model GP Wide-Treads with over-the-hood steering were produced.

Nebraska Test 190: Model GP Wide-Tread
Date: 1931 Fuel: Distillate   HP: 18 Drawbar, 25 Belt

Experimental part numbers are also seen on the BN's front wheel. The heavy wheel and square-headed bolts suggest that this is a wheel weight, but it is really a heavy two-piece wheel. The final wheel design used on production models was much different.

stroke engine, which was followed by the 6-inch bore crossover design. Eventually, that was replaced with the 6-inch bore with a left-side vertical air intake stack and right-side exhaust and muffler. A GPWT with a 6x6-inch bore and stroke was tested at Nebraska in 1931. Test number 190, it was conducted with distillate fuel and yielded 18 drawbar and 25 belt horsepower.

In 1932, the over-the-hood steering replaced the side-steer design. A new seat, moved forward (11-1/2 inches) over the rear axle and raised higher (9-1/2 inches) above an optional operator's platform, increased operator comfort. Other improved features included repositioned throttle and spark controls, a frame that was 6 inches longer, and a

As of 1935, rubber tires had only been available on farm tractors for three or four years, yet farmers were quick to realize that more rubber on the ground meant better traction. These 7.00x40-inch duals were intended to give the 1935 Model B extra pulling power. They were manufactured by French & Hecht but available through Deere dealerships.

INTERNATIONAL HARVESTER McCORMICK-DEERING FARMALL REGULAR: 1924-1932

International Harvester (IH) forever changed the concept of small row-crop tractors with the 1924 introduction of its tricycle Farmall. After viewing a prototype in 1922, management stipulated that the new tractor must be, above all, able to cultivate corn and handle row crop. Therefore, mounted cultivators, corn planters, mowers, and middlebreaker attachments were developed to complement the new tractors.

In large part due to the Farmall's success, in 1925 the company purchased what was once billed as the largest tractor plant in the world, the Moline Plow Company's factory at Rock Island, Illinois. The plant was dedicated solely to the production of the Farmall tractor. By April 12, 1930, the company had produced 100,000 Farmall tractors.

Fitted with an IH vertical, valve-in-head four-cylinder engine that displaced 220-ci from a 3-3/4x5-inch bore and stroke rated at 1,200 rpm, the Farmall developed 13 drawbar and 20 belt horsepower during its 1925 Nebraska Test 117. The test was conducted on kerosene, although the engine was capable of using gasoline as fuel. Its three-speed transmission offered forward travel at 2, 3, and 4 miles per hour, reverse at 2-3/4 miles per hour. The vehicle weighed 3,650 pounds. The Farmall went on the market at a price of $825, and the cultivator listed at $88.50. IH avoided the three-row design and offered two-row or four-row equipment. Production ended in 1932 after an impressive run of approximately 134,650 units were produced.

> **Nebraska Test 117: Farmall Regular**
> **Date: 1925   Fuel: Kerosene   HP: 13 Drawbar, 20 Belt**

Model P: 1930 Only

The Model P Series was a low-production specialty unit built for the potato growers of Maine. These "potato" tractors were assigned separate serial numbers, from P 5000 through P 5202. They carried the same engine as the GP Standard, with a 5-3/4 x6-inch bore and stroke.

What made the P Series GPWT a potato tractor was a 68-inch rear-axle tread, making it possible for the unit to fit the row spacing of the potato fields. The P model came with 8-inch-wide rear wheels with 16 lugs instead of the 10-inch, 24-lug wheels of the regular GPWT tractors.

It doesn't sparkle like its restored kin, but this 1935 Model B with a four-bolt pedestal and dual rear wheels has plenty of charm. The owner knows of only two items that aren't original: the exhaust stack and the magneto. The original magneto is being rebuilt.

The 150 Ps in the initial production run were built as new units, while the remaining ones were rebuilt GP Standard tractors. Eventually, inset rear wheels were developed for the GPWT, which gave it the required 68-inch tread potato farming required, and the P Series was discontinued.

MODEL GPO: 1931–1935

Orchard owners also wanted to retire their horses in favor of the new trend in power farming, but in order to work around and between the trees, orchard farming required a smaller model with a low profile. Responding to this need, the Lindeman Power Equipment Company of Yakima, Washington, modified six Model GP Standards to produce the initial John Deere Orchard and Grove tractors.

The Lindeman modifications lowered the tractor some 7 inches. Deere liked the idea and designed a lower front axle and reversed the rear axle housing to lower the unit, which resulted in the production John Deere GPO Orchard and Grove tractors.

The first six GPOs were converted from Wide-Treads and used the crossover air intake that was featured when the engine bore was increased to 6 inches. Optional fender skirts covered the rear wheels to below the hubs and extended over the flywheel and belt pulley. A radiator guard and curtains were standard equipment, and although the GPO was introduced on steel, rubber tires became an option in 1932.

These John Deere GPO Orchard and Grove tractors were assigned serial numbers 15000 through 15732. The GPOs were not tested at Nebraska.

MODEL GPO-LINDEMAN: 1933–1934

Following the success of the GPO, the Lindeman Company purchased a number of standard-tread GPs and fitted them with a crawler undercarriage. These orchard crawlers became known as the GPO-Lindemans.

Since the powerplant was the same as that used in the GP, the engine stats were the same. Only about 25 units were manufactured by Lindeman-John Deere, and several of these have been found, rescued, and restored by collectors.

MODEL B GENERAL PURPOSE UNSTYLED: 1935–1937

Deere's smaller copy of the extremely popular Model A, the Model B, was considered a two-thirds version of

It stands only 52-1/2 inches high, with shields over the air intake and fuel tank caps. It must be a BO—a 1936 brass-tag, first-year-production BO on full steel.

the Model A in size and power. Deere & Company advertised that the Model A would replace 8 to 10 horses on a working farm, while the Model B was capable of replacing 6 to 8.

More than 306,000 Model Bs were sold during its lifetime, making it the highest-volume production tractor in Deere history. If each tractor replaced four horses, the Model B put approximately 1,224,000 horses out to pasture–or to less desirable fates.

The Model B's extreme popularity resulted in many versions until it was replaced by the Model 50 in 1952. The serial numbers for all models and variants of the B row-crop

tractors were intermixed, starting in 1935 with number 1000 and ending in 1952 with number 310772.

The first Model Bs are known as four-bolt tractors, due to the four bolts that secured the front pedestal. The serial numbers of these tractors began with 1000 and ended with 3042. Initially, the Model B's valve-in-head two-cylinder engine was a 4-1/4x5-1/4-inch bore and stroke, rated at 1,150 rpm. Because of the small engine, no decompression cocks were used. The engine featured a force-feed lubrication system and oil filter. A separate gasoline tank allowed the Model B to be started on gasoline and switched to lower-cost kerosene, tractor fuel, or distillate, once the engine was

T he downward-directed exhaust is another feature that helps identify an orchard model. In this case, it's a 1936 BO. A total of 5,083 copies of the BO were manufactured.

warmed up. A four-speed transmission was standard from the B's introduction until 1941.

Another characteristic of the Bs produced from introduction in 1935 until 1937 was the short frame. Then in 1937, starting with serial number 42200, the frame was lengthened 5 inches to accommodate mid-mounted equipment originally designed for the Model A tractor. The long frame resulted in several changes to the Model B's look and function. Affected were the hood, fuel tank, steering shaft, exhaust pipe, carburetor intake, and drawbar. The very early Bs also featured centerline fuel tank filler caps, which were present from the beginning of production to serial number

INTERNATIONAL HARVESTER McCORMICK-DEERING FARMALL REGULAR: 1932-1938

I nternational Harvester (IH) built on the success of the original Farmall by introducing the first of the F Series, the three-plow F-30, in 1931. The following year, the two-plow F-20 joined the line along with the F Series Farmall, an even smaller, one-plow F-12.

Rear-wheel adjustment from 44 to 78 inches gave the F-12 an almost unlimited application for any row-crop width. Although it was small, the F-12 could handle two-row cultivators and planters. In fact, 15 implements were designed specifically for the F-12. Fitted with an external gear pump on the left side of the transmission, it brought hydraulic muscle and convenience to farm work.

The IH-built four-cylinder valve-in-head engine displaced 113-ci from a 3x4-inch bore and stroke rated at 1,400 rpm. The fuel choices were gasoline or kerosene. The tricycle tractor weighed 2,500 to 2,700 pounds. In 1937, the price for a new Farmall F-12 on steel was $595.

From the first Farmall Regular in 1924 through November 1936, the Farmall colors were gray with red wheels. Following November 1936, the gray color was changed to red, which later led the IH tractor line to be known as Big Red.

> Nebraska Test 220: Farmall F-12
> Date: 1933 Fuel: Kerosene HP: 11 Drawbar, 14 Belt
> Nebraska Test 212: Farmall F-12
> Date: 1933 Fuel: Gasoline HP: 12 Drawbar, 16 Belt

This automobile is a 1918 Model 38 Velie five-passenger touring car with a six-cylinder Continental flathead engine. The Velie automobile company was started by John Deere's grandson. The tractor is a 1936 BO.

1509. Finally, for Model Bs manufactured the first production year, a radiator curtain was standard, and a radiator guard was available as an option. At serial number 34952, shutters replaced the radiator curtain as standard equipment.

John Deere's lower-and-lift-only hydraulic system, which was first introduced on the Model A in early 1933, was available on the Model B when production started late in 1934 (considered 1935 models). An electric starter and electric lights also became available as an option in 1939. The 7-inch headlights were the same as the offered option on the Model D. In addition, selective control of the rockshaft or a double-acting remote cylinder was provided, via the Powr-Trol, which was placed in production August 1, 1945.

Depending on the variant, the Model B weighed approximately 2,455 to 2,765 pounds. Rubber tires were an option from the start of production. The rear tread was adjustable from 56 to 80 inches.

A note of interest is that in 1941, the Model B on steel listed for $750 and on rubber $979, while in 1947 the price had dropped to $597 on steel and $745 on rubber.

> **Nebraska Test 232: Model B**
> **Date: 1935 Fuel: Distillate HP: 11 Drawbar, 16 Belt**

MODEL B GENERAL PURPOSE
EARLY STYLED: 1939–1946

Industrial designer Henry Dreyfuss completed styling for the Model B in 1937, and the new look was introduced in the fall of 1938. Along with the new styling, the bore and stroke was increased to 4-1/2x51/2, which upped the displacement to 174-ci.

Nebraska test number 305, conducted in 1938 on a Model B with the new, larger engine, pegged the results on steel at 14 drawbar and 18 belt horsepower. Running on rubber, the numbers were 16 drawbar and 18 belt horsepower. The tests were conducted using distillates as fuel.

In 1941, two additional forward gears were added to rubber-tired row-crop models. During the war years, when rubber was in short supply, many Model B tractors were produced with steel wheels. In this case, the two extra gears were not added to the transmission. However, many owners later added the two extra gears when their tractors could be fitted with rubber tires.

A 1945 BR, serial number 334377. The BR was never styled, and some collectors consider it ugly. However, hitched to a two-bottom (14-inch) plow, it could plow an acre an hour, and that was beautiful to horse and mule farmers.

> **Nebraska Test 305: Model B Early Styled**
> **Date: 1938 Fuel: Distillate HP: 16 Drawbar**
> **   (on rubber), 18 Belt**

> **Nebraska Test 366: Model B (6/1 transmission)**
> **Date: 1941 Fuel: Distillate HP: 18 Drawbar, 20 Belt**

Tests on a Model B with the new 6/1 transmission were begun at Nebraska in late 1940 but weren't finished until the spring of 1941. Thus, test number 366 is listed as a 1941 test. The six-speed tranny was a three-speed with a second gear-shift lever providing a high-low side to the three basic gears. With distillates as fuel, the results were 18 drawbar and 20 belt horsepower. Deere's new hydraulic system, Powr-Trol, was an option beginning in late 1945.

Styled models of the B gained about 115 pounds over the unstyled models, which boosted the basic weight to 2,878 pounds.

MODEL B LATE STYLED: 1947–1952

The Model B's second-generation styling included an enclosed flywheel, a new seat, a pressed-steel frame, and an electric starter and lights as standard equipment. More user-friendly controls were mounted on the left side of a redesigned steering column pedestal, and the battery was relocated under the cushioned seat. This new generation of Model B tractors, called late-styled, began with serial number 201000.

Along with the styling improvemens, the horsepower was boosted by increasing the bore to 4-11/16 inches, while the stroke remained 5-1/2 inches. The engine produced 190-ci, and the rpm was upped to 1,250.

Engines in the all-fuel and gasoline models of the late-styled Model B tractors were equipped with different pistons, and thus gave different compression ratios, so two separate Nebraska tests were run in 1947. Test number 380 was conducted with gasoline as fuel, and it yielded 24 drawbar and 27 belt horsepower. Nebraska test number 381 was conducted with tractor fuel and produced 21 drawbar and 23 belt horsepower. The tractor for both tests had the 6/1 transmission.

Nebraska Test 380: Model B Late Styled
Date: 1947 Fuel: Gasoline   HP: 24 Drawbar, 27 Belt

Nebraska Test 381: Model B Late Styled
Date: 1947 Fuel: Tractor Fuel HP: 21 Drawbar, 23 Belt

The unstyled, early-styled, and late-styled model variations of the Model B follow.

Equipped with lights, starter, and turning brakes, this "factory correct" 1947 Model BR is serial number 337123. During its working life, it probably never looked this good at day's end.

The working end of a BR shows the PTO shaft, rear light, and the seat with a proper safety decal. It's way too clean to have just done a day's work in the field.

Model BN: 1935–1952

Initially advertised as a garden tractor, the single-front-wheel Model BN was designed for vegetable growers who planted in 28-inch rows or less. The Model BN shared the same specs as the Model B and underwent the same engine and transmission changes during its lifetime. The unstyled Model BN four-bolt model is a rare tractor, of which there were only 24 produced. Approximately 1,001 unstyled Model BNs were built.

Model BW: 1935–1952

Another first-year production Model B variation was the BW, which was fitted with a wide front axle. The four-bolt pedestal was replaced with the eight-bolt design by the time

INTERNATIONAL HARVESTER McCORMICK-DEERING FARMALL H: 1939-1953

With the help of strong sales from the F Series Farmall tractors, International Harvester (IH) weathered the depression years and in 1939 introduced the second generation of the Farmall family. Four models comprised the new line: the small A, the small B, the midsized H, and the large M. The A and B were considered a totally new size of tractor, while the H replaced the F-12 and the M replaced the F-20.

Not only did the new models have advanced and improved mechanical features, IH hired industrial designer Raymond Loewy to give the new Farmalls completely new, modern styling.

The H initially was offered with a choice of steel or rubber tires. A five-speed transmission was standard for the H, although those rolling on steel had the fifth gear locked out. The extra gear gave a transport speed of just over 16 miles per hour for the rubber-tired models. IH's Lift-All hydraulic system was available for the H tractor, but was transmission-activated, and therefore not "live."

The H tractors were powered by a vertical valve-in-head, sleeved, four-cylinder engine, which displaced 152-ci. The engine had a 3-3/8-inch bore with a 4-1/4-inch stroke. The IH-built four-banger was rated at 1,650 rpm. Fuel could be either gasoline, distillate, or kerosene, thanks to an adjustable heat control manifold for burning the low-volatility distillates or kerosene. The rear-wheel tread was adjustable from 44 to 80 inches, which made the tractor a very versatile row-crop machine. A tricycle or standard front axle were offered, along with a full line of implements designed specifically for the H.

The weight on the H is hard to pin down. Nebraska test number 333 listed the H as weighing in at 5,375 pounds, which seems extremely high, considering Nebraska test number 492 lists the Super H as weighing only 4,389 pounds. Brent Sampson of the Nebraska Test Lab explained that the test weight listed for test number 333 included 1,288 pounds of ballast. Remove that, and the tractor weight decreases to a more believable 4,087 pounds.

The H and M were produced at the Farmall Works in Rock Island, Illinois. The 1940 price tag for an H on all-steel was $765, while full-rubber tires ran the bill up to $962.

Nebraska Test 333: Farmall H

Date: 1939   Fuel: Gasoline   HP: 24 Drawbar, 26 Belt

This 1946 BO-Lindeman crawler is equipped with a Lindeman tool-bar/dozer attachment. The Lindeman tool bar could be used as a dozer on the front or turned around and used as a tool bar for implements on the back.

the Model BW was introduced, and its engine and powertrain specs were the same as the Standard Model B.

Model BW-40: 1936 Only

To produce a standard-tread tractor that could work row crops planted in 40-inch rows, six Model BWs were modified to create the Model BW-40. The most significant adjustment was that both the front and rear axles were shortened to produce its very narrow tread. These vehicles were created from the BW, and the engine and drivetrain shared the BW stats.

Model BNH Hi-Clearance: 1937–1946

Late in 1937, greater clearance was created for the Model BN by using larger wheels and tires. The standard front wheel was replaced with a 16-inch rim and the 36-inch rear rims where changed to 40-inch rims. The larger wheels and rubber tires elevated the tractor's stance enough for it to be designated a Hi-Clearance vehicle. The BNH received the early styling and, as it was discontinued in 1946, did not receive the late styling of the 1947 models.

The BWH-40's high clearance and narrow tread are apparent from the camera's low angle. This stance fitted bedded crops in 40-inch rows, and there was over 22 inches of clearance under the front axle.

MINNEAPOLIS-MOLINE TWIN CITY KT: 1929-1934

Three farm implement companies that were hard hit by the tractor price wars and the depressed economy of the 1920s solved the problem by joining forces rather than remaining as competition. In 1929 the Moline Implement Company (MIC), Minneapolis Steel and Machinery Company (MS&M), and Minneapolis Threshing Machine Company (MTM) merged to form the Minneapolis-Moline Power Implement Company (MM).

Although MS&M produced the Twin City tractors and MTM manufactured the Minneapolis line of tractors, the KT—the Kombination Tractor—was the first tractor produced wholly by MM. However, it did retain the Twin City name and gray paint.

The KT was MM's first answer to the market's demand for a small row-crop vehicle that could do a combination of jobs and chores around the farmstead. Like the John Deere Model GP, the KT was designed for a three-row front-mounted cultivator with an arched front axle to give greater clearance for the row the tractor straddled.

It was powered by a four-cylinder 283-ci, valve-in-head, MM-built KE engine with a 4-1/4x5-inch bore and stroke rated at 1,000 rpm. The 3/1 transmission allowed forward speeds ranging from 2.1 to 4.15 miles per hour. The engine could burn either gasoline or kerosene. The KT weighed in at approximately 4,300 pounds.

A KT Orchard Model was offered from 1929 to 1934, while the industrial Model KT-I was produced from 1932 to 1935. In 1934, a new KT rolling on steel listed at $845. Only 2,078 KTs were produced before it was upgraded to the KTA in 1935.

Nebraska Test 175: MM Twin City KT

Date: 1930 Fuel: Kerosene   HP: 18 Drawbar, 25 Belt

Model BWH: 1937–1946

The same changes that applied to the Model BNH changed the Model BW into a Hi-Clearance wide-tread row-crop tractor. The BWH gained rear-axle crop clearance by using the same rear axle as the BNH. A modified BW front axle was used to increase clearance under the BWH's front axle. The spindles were lengthened and more width adjustment was provided. The BWH also only received the early styling, as it, too, was discontinued in 1946.

Model BWH-40: 1939–1941

Fitted with a narrow rear axle, the Model BWH was transformed into a Hi-Clearance tractor for bedded crops in 40-inch rows. Clearance under the front axle was 22-7/8 inches. This rare model didn't make the transformation to the late-styled tractors.

Model BR: 1935–1947

The various row-crop versions of the Model B gave Deere good coverage in that market, but it lacked a small standard tractor to round out the B Series line. That changed in the summer of 1935 with the production of the cute—or ugly, depending on your viewpoint—Model BR, which made an excellent primary tractor for the small farmer or a secondary tractor for larger farm operations.

Only 12 copies of the Model BWH-40 were produced and most, if not all, were shipped to California, where the present owner found this one and brought it back to Nebraska corn country. This 1940 model carries serial number 94435.

"A John Deere with a Swedish accent," is how the owner describes this Swedish-built copy of a Model B John Deere. It isn't an exact copy—all of the parts are slightly different, probably to circumvent patent problems. The Swedish manufacturer called it a Model GMW 25 and gave it serial number TA 2570. Approximately 250 copies were produced.

CASE MODEL CC: 1929-1939

" C " is for cultivator when added to the Case Model C tractor. The Model CC was Case's response to market demand for a smaller general-purpose tractor that was primarily aimed at row-crop farming. The Model CC was designed specifically for that market, and management insisted that a line of mounted equipment be designed along with the tricycle tractor. This concept was viewed as so important that Model CCs were often packaged and sold with a set of "duplex" cultivators—the Model CC mounted one set of shovels on the front and another set was rear-mounted, hence duplex cultivation. Three additional implements were available specifically for the CC: a planter, mower, and middlebuster.

To arrive at the final cultivator tractor, Case engineers modified the Model L design. Specifically, they lengthened the wheelbase, added larger rear wheels, and changed the front axle to tricycle design. An adjustable rear-wheel tread gave the Model CC four-row cultivation and planting capabilities. It wasn't until the mid-1930s that the armstrong lift could be replaced with a mechanical motor lift for raising and lowering mounted equipment.

Variations of the Model CC included high-clearance, wide-row for bedded crops; narrow tread for vineyards and sugar cane; the Florida Special for orchard work; and a high-crop cane tractor. The Case-manufactured four-cylinder vertical, I-head, valve-in-head engine displaced 259-ci from a 4-7/8x5-1/2-inch bore and stroke. Capable of burning either kerosene or gasoline, it was rated at 1,100 rpm. The three-speed tranny provided forward travel at 2-5/8, 3-3/4, or 5-1/8 miles per hour. The Model CC weighed approximately 4,090 pounds. It was manufactured at the J. I. Case Tractor Plant in Racine, Wisconsin. The production numbers during its lifetime totaled 28,652 vehicles.

In 1939, its last year of production, you could take home a steel-wheeled Model CC for $975.

> **Nebraska Test 169: Case Model CC**
> **Date: 1929 Fuel: Kerosene HP: 22 Drawbar, 28 Belt**

The Model BR started life with the same engine and transmission as the other B tractors, but the BR's manifold was a departure from the regular B design. Although the intake passage and location of the carburetor remained the same, an orchard-type muffler was used. This allowed the exhaust/muffler to be directed upward, downward, or horizontally to the front or rear.

The engine displacement and horsepower were increased in 1939, as the bore and stroke was changed from 4-1/4x4-1/4 (149ci) to 4-1/2x5-1/2 (174-ci). Cylinder decompression cocks were standard on the larger engine.

The BR's 115-inch overall length (68-inch wheelbase) was shorter than other B models. In order to achieve a 12-gallon fuel capacity with the shorter fuel tank, the tank was widened and the tapered hood eliminated.

The BR was available with a wide selection of tire and wheel options in either steel or rubber. Steel came in round-spoke 5.00x24-inch for the front and flat-spoke 8.00x40-inch for the rear. Rubber tire options were round-spoke 5.50x16-inch front and either 11.25x24-inch or 9.00/10.00x28-inch cast rear, or 11.25x24-inch round-spoke rear. The customer could mix and match steel and rubber if preferred.

In 1942, the rear size was changed to the 11.00x26-inch, which was standard until 1947, when production ended for the Model BR. The Model BO and BR tractors were assigned

Parked nose-to-nose, the differences between a Model B John Deere and the Swedish GMW 25 become apparent. The GMW was manufactured in 1955.

serial numbers 325000 through 337514, between 1936 and 1947. They were never styled by Henry Dreyfuss and his team of industrial designers.

Model BO: 1935–1947

Only a few changes were required to turn the Model BR into an orchard vehicle. The Model BO retained the same overall size as the BR, but without the vertical air intake stack it stood only 52-1/2 inches tall. Shields over the air intake, gasoline tank cap, and fuel tank cap prevented limbs from catching as the tractor worked close to the fruit trees. In addition, full citrus fenders that covered the rear wheels to below the axle were available as an option. The orchard version of the BR was a respectable seller, with 5,083 produced during its lifetime.

In June 1938, the 4-1/4x5-1/4-inch bore and stroke engine was replaced with the larger 4-1/2x5-1/2-inch bore and stroke design.

Model BO-L: 1939–1947

One John Deere Model BO chassis, minus the wheel equipment and front axle, plus a Lindeman track assembly, equals one nifty little crawler.

Production of Model BO Crawlers from the Lindeman plant totaled 1,645 units, plus 29 BRs and one BI.

Model BI: 1936–1941

A highway-yellow paint job with black lettering was the most visible change that distinguished a B Series standard-tread from an industrial Model BI. The Model BR and BI had major components in common. However, the BI had its front axle set back 5-1/4-inches, reducing the wheelbase from 68 to 62-3/4-inches. The front frame was machined, drilled, and tapped to facilitate the mounting of industrial equipment.

Several changes were made to accommodate the heavier loads anticipated with industrial work, including a beefier drawbar and larger outer bearing on the rear axle. Other modifications included a padded seat, fixed to a channel iron support that was mounted to the rear axle housing. The air stack was lower than that on the BR tractor. When the BI was equipped with rubber tires, individual rear breaks were standard.

The Model BI serial numbers fell within the standard-tread Model B numbers.

ALLIS-CHALMERS MODEL RC 1939–1941

Allis-Chalmers' (AC) line of tractors had a void between its small, highly successful Model B and the larger, even more popular Model WC. Allis-Chalmers aimed to fill this void with its new Model RC, a two-row tractor. But AC didn't exactly hit the bull's-eye, as only about 5,500 units were produced.

Where did AC go wrong? Though the company managed to fill a slot in its tractor line until the Model C debuted the following year, the Model RC was overweight and underpowered, the result of combining the WC chassis with a smaller 125-ci engine. The RC was equipped to use most of the WC's mounted equipment. It utilized the same PTO, belt pulley, and mechanical power lift as the WC, and it was less expensive, but again it was a case of too much weight and not enough power.

The powerplant was an Allis-Chalmers vertical I-head four-cylinder with 3-3/8x3-1/2-inch bore and stroke that turned out 1,500 rpm. It could use either gasoline or kerosene as fuel. The RC's four-speed transmission could pull the load, but at a much slower speed. The test weight is listed as 2,495 pounds on steel or 3,204 pounds on rubber. The WC test weight was 2,700 pounds on steel or 3,300 pounds on rubber. Obviously, the RC was packing almost as much weight as the higher-powered WC.

The price for a first-year 1939 Model RC listed at $690 on steel, while it took $810 to purchase one on rubber. A year later, the WC on steel was priced at $995, or $1,240 fitted with rubber tires. The RC saved a farmer a few bucks when he traded in his horse or mule team for this new tractor.

For certain, all of the hoofed trade-ins during those days caused some major changes at the tractor dealerships. According to Fred Hileman, former director of service in the marketing division, the burgeoning tractor business resulted in dealerships constructing corrals, providing oats and hay, and removing manure in order to accommodate the many "broom tails" that were traded in on a new tractor.

> Nebraska Test 316: Allis-Chalmers Model RC
> Date: 1939 Fuel: Distillate HP: 15 Drawbar, 18 Belt

Chapter 2

FOUR- TO SIX-HORSE TRACTORS

Models H and M

With the growing success of the Models A and B, Deere & Company's tractor program was advancing nicely. But there were still strong competitors with strong products, and all were vying for the lion's share of the "horse" market.

The Model H was introduced in 1939, the same year that Henry Ford and Harry Ferguson showcased their revolutionary new Ford 9N with the Ferguson hydraulic system and three-point hitch. Sales numbers on the little gray tractors were what the rest of the industry could only dream about. During the war years, when Deere and many other manufacturers discontinued production of many models, the new Ford-Ferguson 9N and 2N racked up sales, totaling almost 200,000 units by the end of the conflict in 1945.

Previous pages

This wagon, with original John Deere decals and lettering, could have originated in one of three manufacturing facilities from which Deere & Company manufactured or outsourced wagons: Moline Wagon Company, Moline, Illinois; Fort Smith Wagon Company, Fort Smith, Arkansas; or the Davenport Wagon Company, Davenport, Iowa.

MODEL H: 1939–1947

The Model H was an "a little less than, a little more than" tractor. A little less power and cost than the Model B, but a little more power and cost than the Model L. And the Model H was capable of doing a lot more work than any team of horses. Deere's advertising literature for the Model H informed potential buyers that the two-row tractor could cultivate 25 to 30 acres of row crop per day, compared to only 8 acres per day with a one-row horse-drawn cultivator.

Deere & Company Decision No. 7900, dated September 29, 1938, set out the rationale and specifications for the Model H tractor:

> To meet the needs of small farms for limited power at low cost and for supplemental power on large farms, we will authorize the production of a lighter General Purpose Tractor designated as the Model H with the following features:
>
> I. Low Production Cost, obtained by:
> A. Low material cost resulting from extensive use of high-strength materials and simplification of design, with a net dry weight of approximately 2,070 lbs.
> B. Low labor cost secured through reduction in total number of parts and in simplification of parts.
> II. Low Operating Cost, which results from:
> A. Low fuel consumption due to power requirement closely approximating the economical load range of the engine.
> B. The use of a two-cylinder variable-speed engine adapted to low-cost fuels.
> C. Decreased rolling resistance due to light weight, large diameter wheels and the use of rubber tires on rear and front wheels.

Other features listed provided tread adjustment from 44 to 80 inches for working all row crop planted in rows spaced up to 42 inches; a three-speed transmission; the ability to use low-cost, quick-detachable integral tools; improved vision and comfort; individual steering brakes; and styling comparable to the Models A and B tractors with a design to accentuate ruggedness and strength.

Another all-important criterion for the Model H tractor was a low price tag—within the budget of approximately

This 1941 HNH is 1 of only 37 copies ever manufactured. Extra crop clearance under the rear axle was achieved by replacing the 7x32 rear wheels with 8x38 wheels. California's vegetable farming region was the destination of most HNH vehicles.

four million small farmers who, manufacturers hoped, wanted to trade in their horses for mechanical horsepower. Many of these farmers had 80 acres or less in crops, of which almost 25 percent went to feed the four-legged hay burners—their horses and livestock. It was a market whose potential had captured the attention of Deere management, as well as its competition.

Small-tractor concepts were explored at the Moline, Illinois, facility from the early 1930s under the direction

It has no doubt been many years since this HNH worked the vegetable fields of California. But, with the single front wheel, ample rear axle clearance, and adjustable rear tread, it's easy to see that's where it would shine.

MASSEY-HARRIS CHALLENGER MODEL CH (UNSTYLED) 1936-1937

The best year for tractor production during the first half of the twentieth century was 1929, when the industry cranked out 229,000 units. In 1936, tractor manufacturers recorded their second-best year, with 227,185 new tractors produced.

In addition, 1936 was the year Massey-Harris (M-H) fielded its first row-crop tractor, called the Challenger. The Challenger retained the boilerplate frame from the tractor that it was replacing, the 12-20 Wallis tractor. Its over-the-hood steering was similar to the steering on many Deere General Purpose models.

Powered by an all-fuel M-H-built four-cylinder I-head engine with 3-7/8x5-1/4-inch bore and stroke, it was rated at 1,200 rpm. The transmission was a 4/1 with forward speeds of 2- 7/16, 3-1/3, 4, and 8-1/2 miles per hour. The Challenger sported a dark green engine and chassis, dark red wheels, and a yellow lettering color scheme. The company advertised the Challenger as a 2-3 plow row-crop tractor with the rear tread width adjustable from 52 to 80 inches. The standard front axle was the dual front-wheel tricycle, with a wide adjustable offered as an option. The buyer could choose accessory items such as an American Bosch U4 magneto, Kingston carburetor, Handy governor, and rubber tires or steel wheels.

The unit on steel weighed about 3,520 pounds and sold for $1,025. On rubber, the price bounced up to $1,220.

> **Nebraska Test 265: Massey-Harris Challenger Model CH (Unstyled)**
>
> **Date: 1936   Fuel: Distillate   HP: 20 Drawbar, 28 Belt**

of chief engineer Max Sklovsky. Moline's experimental department produced the Model Y, the Model 62, and the Model L, from 1935 through 1937.

The Waterloo facility began work on its own small experimental tractor sometime in 1937, which resulted in the Model H. The first prototypes, or experimental vehicles, carried the designation XO and were unstyled, bare-bones renderings. The front steering pedestal and steering post were slanted toward the rear of the tractor, and cast-iron rear wheels were of a five-star design. Both features gave these experimental tractors a unique appearance.

Extensive field testing during the summer of 1938 confirmed that the tractor was ready for production, which began in December 1938. However, the production line had barely begun to roll when the decision was made to change the cast-iron alloy crankshaft to a forged-steel crankshaft for increased strength. Most of the first 104 tractors manufactured with the cast-iron crankshaft were retrofitted with the new forged-steel crank.

Power for the Model H, in all variants, was provided by a Deere-built two-cylinder horizontal engine with 3-9/16x5-inch bore and stroke, for 100-ci displacement. It was an all-fuel engine cooled by thermosiphon, and was wound

The HWH is another version of the Model H, and this 1941 HWH is 1 of only 126 made. The pressed-steel rear wheels have a nine-hole bolt pattern—the same as the HNH. The HWH was another California tractor.

a little tighter than the previous Deere tractors, with a rated speed of 1,400 rpm.

Although the two-cylinder engine design was true-Deere horizontal, it did have one notable difference, as noted in Deere & Company Decision No. 7900: "The transmission is of the all spur gear type, employing but three steps of reduction. The design differs from that of the Models A, B, and G, in that power is taken from the cam shaft of the engine rather than the crankshaft, thereby taking advantage of the 2-to-1 speed reduction from the crankshaft to camshaft, and affording quiet operation due to the low velocity of the belt pulley gear. The use of this three-speed transmission with the variable-speed engine provides a wide range of speeds adapted to all farm purposes."

Danny Gleeson, a retired Deere engineer, pointed out that the Model H never changed bore and stroke or horsepower during its years of production. Gleeson also passed on a tip for restorers dealing with frozen engines: Pouring Coca-Cola in the cylinders will free up stuck pistons.

Another feature that remained constant throughout the Model H's lifetime was a three-speed transmission that rolled it forward at 2-1/2, 3-1/2, or 5-3/4miles per hour. To make road travel from field to field faster, a foot throttle revved up the engine rpm to 1,800 and the travel speed to 7-1/2 miles per hour. The dry weight for the basic Model H was 2,054 pounds, while the Model HWH tipped the scales at 2,354 pounds.

Some of the mounted, or integral, equipment designed for the Model H included a one-way plow, a two-way plow, two-row planters, single- and double-row cultivators, sweep rake, and vegetable-harvesting equipment.

Hydraulic power became available for the Model H tractors in late 1940, and it could be integrated as a factory or field installation. Buyers also could order a number of optional items to customize a Model H to their specific farming needs, such as an electrical system for a starter and lights, just a starter, or just lights. A radiator shutter was offered instead of the standard curtain plus a power shaft (PTO) with shield. Fenders were also an option.

By 1941, the year this HWH was manufactured, the horse and mule population had dwindled to half of what it had been in 1918. John Deere wagons, like the one in the foreground, were nearly obsolete.

According to Deere Company's decision book, the first serial number for the Model H was H-1000, and the final number was 61116, though not all of the serial number plates were used. The actual production was 57,363 vehicles, with production beginning in 1938, and concluding on February 6, 1947.

Ah, the good ol' days! This nostalgic scene is what tractor manufacturers were determined to eradicate. Consider that it would take all day to plow a mere 2 acres, and the temperature was 107 degrees. It's easy to see how Model H tractors would be an easy sell.

Production of the Model H tricycle accounted for 57,363 vehicles. Some Model H serial number plates were not used, so the higher ending serial number (H-61116) gives an incorrect total.

No separate serial numbers were assigned to the HN, HNH, and HWH, and they fell within the Model H numbers. However, the first serial number for each variant is noted. For the HN model, the serial number of the first tractor is H-14874. The starting date of the Model HN is listed as February 19, 1940, and the ending date of February 6, 1947, applies to all Model H tractors.

"Rolling on rubber" was the only way the customer could buy any Model H tractor. When introduced, the Model H standard rear tires were 6.50x32, but 7.50x32 tires were offered as an option. By March, the 7.50x32 had been adopted as the standard-equipment rear tire.

Model HN

The genesis of the Model HN lies in Decision No. 9000, dated January 15, 1940, which read, in part:

> To provide a Model H Tractor which is better adapted to the cultivation of vegetables which are planted in rows of 28 inches or less, we will adopt a single front wheel Model HN General Purpose Tractor. This tractor will be similar to the Model H General Purpose Tractor except that it will be equipped with a single front wheel with 6x12 tire supported by a yoke instead of two front wheels with 4.00x15 tires supported by a double knuckle. The change in the mounting for the single front wheel will require providing a new pedestal assembly.

This adaptation of the Model H was first proposed in October 1939, following the start of production on the H, when the sales department recognized the need for a tractor such as the HN. Patterns and casting flasks for the pedestal and front wheel were to be ready by February 1940, and the first HN was produced on February 19, 1940.

Approximately 1,077 single-front-wheel Model HNs were built.

Model HWH

The first Model HWH was assigned serial number H-29982 when production started on March 5, 1941. Only 126 copies of the Model HWH tractor exited the assembly line.

Two different front axles were ultimately available for the Model HWH. The narrow center section allowed the front wheels to be set for crops planted in narrow rows. The wide

Today, just the harness on this team of Belgian sorrels costs about twice as much as a basic Model H tractor of its time. Tractor manufacturers were right on when they repeatedly pointed out how expensive it was to maintain work horses.

center section front axle allowed wider tread settings for crops planted in 42-inch rows.

The San Francisco Branch was also instrumental in bringing the Model HWH online, according to Deere & Company Decision No. 9800:

> To meet the demands from the field for high-clearance, adjustable-tread front wheels on the Model H Tractor, we will adopt an HWH Tractor, similar to present AWH and BWH Tractors. To obtain additional clearance under the rear axle, we will change rear wheels with tires from 7x32 to 8x38.
>
> These tractors will regularly be equipped with a front axle (short) to give tread range from 40 to 52 inches by increments of 4 inches. A special equipment front axle (long) and drag links will be adopted to give tread range of 56 to 68 inches by 4-inch increments. This can be assembled on the tractor at the factory or furnished separately to users who may desire the full tread range from 40 to 68 inches. The rear wheel tread with the 8x38 tires is the same as for Model H—44 to 84 inches.

Model HNH

By far, the rarest of the H models is the HNH, of which only 37 copies were produced. The beginning serial number for the HNH is H-30172, and the first Model HNH vehicle was produced on March 11, 1941.

Farmers and dealership personnel often influenced product design at Deere & Company, which was the case when the San Francisco Branch proposed the change that resulted in Deere & Company Decision No. 9915:

> To meet requests from the trade (particularly the San Francisco Branch) for more crop clearance under the Rear Axle Housings than that possible with the HN Tractor, we will adopt a Model HNH Tractor by replacing the 7x32 rubber tired wheels (having a rolling radius of 21.1 inches) with the 8x38 size used on the HWH Tractor (having a rolling radius of 25.0 inches). This will provide the same road speeds and crop clearance at the rear as for the HWH model by decision number 9800. The Front End will be 1/32 lower than the rear on the HNH instead of 3-7/8 inches higher than the rear, as in the case of the HN.

This view of the HWH shows the tall axle spindles on the adjustable front axle. The narrower of the two adjustable axles available for the HWH, this one allows a front tread width from 40 to 52 inches.

The owner of this Model H said it was built on December 1, 1941, just six days before Pearl Harbor was bombed. World War II interrupted production of the Model H at least two different times, once in 1942 and again in 1943.

World War II interrupted production of the Model H Series several times—sometimes for as long as 12 months, and no HNH or HWH models were produced after World War II. The base price for the Model H began at $595 plus freight. This was a lot of tractor for the money, and considering Deere & Company invested over $1 million to develop the Model H, it would take a lot of sales to recover its investment.

> Nebraska Test 312: Model H
> Date: 1938 Fuel: Distillate   HP: 12 Drawbar, 14 Belt

During Nebraska Test 312, the Model H set a fuel-economy performance record of 11.95 horsepower hours per gallon of distillate.

It quickly became apparent to Deere, and the competition, that features that would meet or exceed those of the Ford-Ferguson 9N, such as electric lights, electric start, low cost, and most of all, advanced hydraulics to handle integral, or mounted equipment, must be rolled out immediately.

Fortunately, Deere had just such a tractor on the drawing board. It was the Model M.

MODEL M: 1946–1952

World War II had a significant impact on tractor production and development for all manufacturers. War materiel had first priority for production facilities, raw material was rationed, and no new tractor models could go into production. However, Deere & Company President C. D. Wiman considered research and development critical to the company, and he ordered R & D to continue throughout the war years.

The Model M General Purpose Utility was the replacement for the Models L and LA. Introduced in 1946, the Model M was to become Deere's small tractor that was specifically aimed at replacing the remaining horse and mule workforce. With approximately 87,812 copies produced, it certainly replaced a lot of work animals.

ALLIS-CHALMERS MODEL B 1937-1957

Allis-Chalmers' (AC) mandate for the Model B was to replace the horses on small family farms. Company advertisements compared the cost of maintaining true horse power to the advantages of the new Model B, stating that it took 5 acres of cropland to feed one horse; thus, maintaining five work horses would require 25 acres of cropland. Why not purchase a Model B and put those 25 acres into profitable crops or livestock?

Apparently, a lot of small farmers agreed. Allis-Chalmers sold 120,783 Model Bs and its variants during its 20 years in the AC lineup. The highest-production year was 1939, when 21,707 vehicles rolled off the production lines.

Industrial designer Brooks Stevens gave the Model B a distinctive look with a slender waist, rounded hood, and wide upholstered seat. Several variants were eventually available, including a Potato Special, Asparagus Special, and the Industrial Model IB. A wide-adjustable front axle became available in 1945, which, coupled with the adjustable rear tread width, gave the Model B great versatility for specialty row-crop cultivation.

Tractors in the initial production run of about 90 Model Bs were fitted with a four-cylinder Waukesha engine with a 3x4-inch bore and stroke that displaced 113-ci. This was replaced in 1938 by an AC-built, 1,400-rpm four-cylinder with a 3-1/4x3-1/2-inch bore and stroke that displaced 116-ci. In 1943, the bore was increased to 3-3/8-inches, which bumped the displacement to 125-ci, and the rpm was upped to 1,500. Forward travel speeds of 2-1/2, 4, and 7-3/4 miles per hour were provided by the standard three-speed transmission.

For the first 10 years of production, the hydraulic system was a raise-and-lower only. The Traction-Booster system was brought online in 1957, and provided depth control for mounted equipment. A full line of farming equipment was designed especially for the Model B, which gave the small farmer the same tools as the large operators.

Conceived as a rubber-tire-only vehicle, some Model Bs were produced on steel during World War II, when rubber was in short supply. A Model B on rubber carried an introductory price tag of $495 in 1938. By the end of production in 1957, the price was $1,440 for a standard front axle Model B. The shipping weight was 1,860 pounds.

Nebraska Test 302: Allis-Chalmers Model B
Date: 1938 Fuel: Distillate   HP: 13 Drawbar, 15 Belt
Nebraska Test 439: Allis-Chalmers Model B
Date: 1950 Fuel: Gasoline   HP: 19 Drawbar, 22 Belt

This tire pump attachment, mounted on a Model H's PTO, was a real time and labor saver—just ask anyone who has ever pumped up a rear tractor tire with a hand pump. The parts book lists this model as first manufactured in 1938.

Hydraulic power came to the Model H on the 1941 models. The hydraulic unit, driven off the engine governor shaft, was live and could operate either one or two remote cylinders. The system could be ordered from the factory or as a dealer-installed option. The parts book shows this power lift system also fit the HN, HNH, and HWH.

Designs and prototypes were developed at the Moline Tractor Works facility in Moline, Illinois, but the actual production of the Model M took place at the new Deere plant in Dubuque, Iowa.

According to Mike Mack, retired director of Waterloo's Product Engineering Center, the following personnel were responsible for engineering the Model M: Willard Nordenson, who was chief engineer at Deere's Dubuque facility and an engine expert who supervised the entire Model M design and build; Dan Mihal, an engineer who was responsi-

ble for designing the transmission for all Model Ms; Dan Hall, the engineer who was in charge of hydraulics for the Model M; and Harold Borsheim, an engineer who worked on the MC Crawler design and was instrumental in launching the industrial effort at the Dubuque plant.

Mack recalls his experiences with development and production of the Model M. "Willard Nordenson and his engineering group were located in Moline when he offered me my first job when I was first out of school. We worked in Moline as an engineering group on the design of the Model M

CASE MODEL V: 1939-1941

Leon R. Clausen was hired by Deere & Company in 1912 and soon advanced to the manager position of Deere's Ottumwa works. In 1919, he was elected to Deere's board of directors and given new responsibility as vice president in charge of all manufacturing operations.

Clausen left Deere & Company in 1924 to assume the presidency of the J. I. Case Threshing Machine Company. His evaluation of the company's tractor operations was as follows: "When I came to Racine, Case's tractor line was obsolete, both in appearance and performance." Clausen was charged with making Case tractors contenders in the marketplace, and, on many occasions, he was responsible for letting many of the competition's engineering advancements beat Case to the marketplace.

With great reluctance, Clausen put aside his opposition to the low-margin small-tractor market. Sales were lost every day because Case didn't have anything to offer small-tractor buyers, and these people were spending their tractor dollars at the competition's dealerships. Case's reputation for well-built products had made it successful in the threshing machine market, and its early tractors were hallmarked by "hell-for-stout" heavy iron. This engineering ideal was reflected in the Model V and Model VA, the anchors of Case's small-tractor line.

The Model V was powered by a four-cylinder Continental engine with a 3x4-3/8-inch bore and stroke rated at 1,425 rpm. The Clark transmission was a four-speed with a low end of 2-1/2 miles per hour and a high end of 9-1/2 miles per hour. The engine rpm was limited to 1,425 in first and second gear, but a transmission interlock linked to the governor allowed 1,600 rpm in third and fourth gear as well as neutral, for belt work. This was dropped when the Model SC was introduced, because the Model V could easily handle a two-bottom plow and the two-plow slot was now SC territory.

The Model V came with both a hand throttle and foot throttle as standard equipment. A starter was not standard equipment, but because the flywheel was fitted with a ring gear, it wasn't difficult to install this option. The less expensive Edison Splitdorf magneto was prone to problems and made hand-cranking a real adventure in patience and profanity.

Steel wheels or rubber tires were available. On steel the price tag was $605. On rubber the price was $645. The row-crop version, the Model VC, with a tricycle front axle and standard rear axle, allowed tread width from 44 to 82 inches.

A low-production variant was the industrial Model VI, which retained the same engine and drivetrain. There was also a single-front-wheel option brought online in 1941. Production ended in October 1941, after 10,245 Model Vs were built.

while the factory was being built in Dubuque. The engineering group moved to Dubuque in July 1947. I believe the tractors started coming off the Dubuque production line in December 1946."

Mack commented on the rationale behind the vertical design of the Model M engine, unusual considering that traditional Deere & Company two-cylinder engines were horizontal. "The biggest reason I can suggest is that Nordenson was his own guy, and he didn't report to the chief engineer or the factory manager over here in Waterloo. There is probably a better explanation than that, but I think when all the smoke clears away, this is what it really boils down to—Nordenson just decided to do his thing, and by making it vertical, it set it a little bit apart, somewhat of a departure from the traditional. This is my belief just from knowing him. The people in Waterloo were regarded by him as a different team,

although the same company, and he didn't report to anybody in Waterloo. He reported to the senior vice president in Moline, as did the people in Waterloo.

"He did other things differently. For years the Waterloo tractors had a hand- operated clutch," Mack continued. "I used to hear Nordenson use the expression, 'I don't think an operator has enough hands to use a hand clutch.' So, he put a conventional foot-operated clutch on the Model M tractor."

Mack went on to explain the development of the hydraulic system that was a standard feature on the Model M from planning to production. "The hydraulics were designed by a fellow by the name of Dan Hall. Dan did

Shown here is another side of the 1950 Model M, serial number 43314. Its 18 drawbar horsepower was one more horse than the Ford 9N, and it had Touch-O-Matic hydraulics, Deere's answer to the Ferguson hydraulic system featured on the 9N.

This 1950 Model MT is 1 of 30,472 MTs manufactured from December of 1948 to September of 1952.

Model MT: 1949–1952

Introduced in 1949, the MT was a row-crop version of the Model M utility tractor. Three front-axle versions were available, including the dual front-wheel tricycle, the wide adjustable, and the single front wheel.

Mack continued by explaining how the Model M variants were developed. "A little later on, Willard Nordenson sold management on the idea of a Model MT, which was a derivative of the Model M, that you could buy with a single front wheel, a two-wheel tricycle, or a wide extended front axle to straddle two rows."

Nebraska Test 423: Model MT

Date: 1949   Fuel: Gasoline   HP: 18 Drawbar, 20 Belt

something unique on the hydraulics. The rockshaft had two telescoping shafts, one inside the other, so you could raise the right side or left side independently. I believe that was a first on Deere tractors."

Mack explained how the Model M stacked up against other John Deere tractors. "The Model M was quite different in almost every respect. We had an engineering group that was totally unrelated to the engineering group in Waterloo. The two chief engineers, well, any way you slice it, it was a competitive situation that developed. People don't like to talk about it but given that kind of an environment, people tend to do their own thing. That engine established Nordenson's reputation. It developed a reputation for being a very, very reliable engine. It was rugged, very long lasting.

"Incidentally, the Model M was Deere's first involvement with spiral bevel gears. Nobody in Deere had ever designed a spiral bevel differential. The engineers at Gleason Works of Rochester, New York, designed and developed the tooling to make a spiral bevel gear in the differential. Deere, of course, bought the tooling and manufacturing equipment from Gleason. That was the first spiral bevel differential that was ever produced by Deere, and now they are all spiral bevels."

The Model M was a mainstay in the John Deere line until 1952.

Nebraska Test 387: Model M

Date: 1947   Fuel: Gasoline   HP: 18 Drawbar, 20 Belt

Model MI: 1949–1952

In order to create a Model MI from the Model M, a new lower front axle design and adjusted final drive housings were required. These changes lowered the tractor some 8 inches and reduced the wheelbase an equal amount.

Mack recalled this about the MI tractors. "The 'I' designated an industrial tractor. The drop housings were rotated 90 degrees forward. Of course, that dropped the whole chassis by the distance of the two gears in the drop housing. That enhanced the stability, which was obviously necessary, because many of these vehicles were involved in a mowing operation on hillsides, so lateral stability was very, very critical.

"John Deere didn't make the belly-mounted mower that was used with the MI. We purchased the mower from a company over in Ohio.

"A lot of these tractors were painted yellow for industrial applications. Incidentally, somebody had the notion that you could take this little old green agricultural tractor and spray yellow paint on it, and that would enhance the structural integrity of that tractor. The implement people immediately started cheating on how much load you could put on those axles. They'd spray it with yellow paint, and then they'd believe you could put a loader on the front end and a backhoe on the rear end and everything would be lovely. They thought that when you sprayed it with yellow paint, the properties of the iron suddenly changed. We learned the hard way that it didn't change. You can imagine what happened to the front axle, and you can imagine what happened to final drive gears and the transmission gears.

"We had to start beefing things up. There was a lot of pressure from marketing to do this. We jumped on that, and got on top of the problem. It was the 1940s, and we were very inexperienced in the yellow business."

The Model M featured a telescoping steering wheel, which could be adjusted to suit each individual operator.

Fully extended, the steering wheel of the Model M would literally be in the operator's lap, but it could be locked into any position desired by the operator.

The seat and front wheels on the Model MT tricycle are both offset to the tractor's right, which makes it easier for operators to see the row while working row crop.

The total Model MI production numbered 1,032 vehicles, and all wore highway orange or industrial yellow with black decals.

Model MC: 1949–1952

Another product of the Dubuque, Iowa, facility was the crawler version of the Model M, which was introduced in 1949. It differed from the previous John Deere crawlers in that it didn't use the Lindeman undercarriage.

Mack recalled how the MC was Dubuque's first dive into the industrial business.

"My recollection of it is that the Lindeman people made a couple of mock-ups and demonstrated them to the brass. Harold Borsheim made the design right there in Dubuque, the design that went into production. It was quite successful in the yellow market. Borsheim became the father of the Model MC and finished his career on the crawler tractors for Deere."

Nebraska Test 448: Model MC
Date: 1950   Fuel: Gasoline   HP: 17 Drawbar, 21 Belt

CASE MODEL VA: 1942-1953

The redesigned Model V debuted as the Model VA in late 1941. Manufactured at Case's Rock Island facility, by February 1942, production was at 300 per week.

Case chose to make this a more vertically integrated manufacturing project by designing and building its own engine and transmission. The engine was designed by Case, but initially it was built by Continental with a mix of its own parts and others furnished by Case. In 1946, the Case engine production line was in operation, and all subsequent engines were wholly Case made. The VA's four-cylinder engine featured a 3-1/4x3-3/4-inch bore and stroke rated at 1,425 rpm, and the Case-built transmission was a four-speed.

The VA line grew to include the Model VA, standard tread; the Model VAO, orchard; the Model VAI, industrial; the VAC, tricycle; the Model VAIH, high-crop special; the VAS, off-center driveline; and a single front-wheel model.

The Ford 9N tractor with the Ferguson system frustrated Case Manager Leon Clausen, who considered it "phony as a three-dollar bill," but its success in the marketplace eventually forced Case to respond with a competing hydraulic system for mounted equipment. The Case system was advertised as the Case Eagle Hitch, and in some ways was probably superior in performance to the Ford-Ferguson three-point system—but not in sales.

The VAC tipped the scales at just over 3,000 pounds and carried a suggested retail price of about $1,500 at the end of production in 1953. The Model V and VA were never tested at Nebraska, but they no doubt carried similar horsepower to the Model VAC.

> **Nebraska Test 430: Case Model VA**
> **Date: 1949 Fuel: Tractor Fuel HP: 15 Drawbar, 17 Belt**

The Model M that never made it into production was the orchard version. Mack explains the development and the reasons why it never became a production vehicle. "We had an orchard tractor, the MO, which never got into production. I was given the job of converting the Model M to an orchard tractor.

"A lot of sheet metal had to be designed to fit over this chassis. It was a lot of fun, a really nifty thing, an exercise in what we call descriptive geometry, because all these shapes and forms were curved with strange shapes. This was before the days of computer graphics, so the whole thing had to be designed manually.

"We made mock-ups of it and tested all these strange metal shapes. The fundamental problem was that the Waterloo facility was building an orchard tractor. We were about to build an orchard tractor. I don't think there was enough volume there to support the investment. The MO really never got past the engineering department."

Deere tractors used the thermosiphon cooling system longer than most other tractor manufacturers. Mack made this the subject of his master's thesis.

Continues on page 58

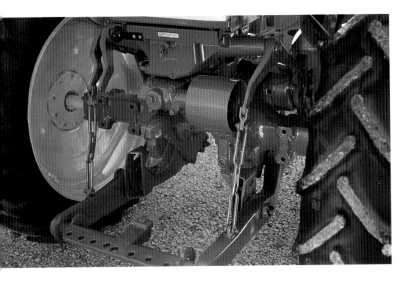

This PTO pulley was one of the options available for the MT. This view also shows the rockshafts and lift arms of the Touch-O-Matic hydraulic system and Quik-Tatch hitch system.

The owner of this 1949 Model MI, serial number 10937, just doesn't like all-yellow tractors, so this piece of machinery could pass as an agricultural vehicle. However, its lower stance is one clue that it is an industrial model of the M.

INTERNATIONAL HARVESTER McCORMICK-DEERING FARMALL MODEL B: 1939-1947

In 1939, International Harvester (IH) introduced a new line of tractors specifically aimed at small-acreage farmers who utilized one or two teams of animal power. The Farmall Models A and B were one-plow tractors capable of one- or two-row cultivation.

Both models were nearly identical, except that the Model A featured a wide-tread front axle, while the Model B was a tricycle tractor, available with either a single- or dual-wheel front axle. The Model BN was an 8-inch narrower version of the Model B that was designed to work closely spaced row crop.

The powerplant for the A, B, and BN was an IH-built four-cylinder with 3x4-inch bore and stroke that displaced 113-ci. Rated rpm was pegged at 1,400. Buyers could choose either the kerosene/distillate version or the higher-compression gasoline engine. The cooling system on the Model A and Model B was thermosiphon. Fitted with a 4/1 transmission, the Model B traveled 2-1/4, 3-5/8, 4-3/4, or 10 miles per hour. The rear-tread adjustment on the Model B was 64 to 92 inches.

The novel and useful design of the Farmall was the offset centerline of the engine and driveline, with the seat on the right, which give the operator a clear view when working row crop. IH called this feature "Culti-Vision." IH's Model B design featured the slender torque tube, which proved too much like Allis-Chalmers' original design and resulted in IH paying Allis for patent infringement.

Another IH innovation was the pneumatic Lift-All for the small Farmalls, including the A, B, and BN. A control lever routed the exhaust pressure through a large cylinder to activate the lift system for raising and lowering mounted equipment. In addition, an electric starter and lights were available either as a factory option or a field conversion, and a line of specially designed implements was available for the Model B. These tractors were built at IH's Chicago Works facility.

The Model B weighed a mere 1,780 pounds, and the base price in 1940 was $605.

Nebraska Test 331: Farmall Model B
Date: 1939 Fuel: Gasoline   HP: 16 Drawbar, 18 Belt
Nebraska Test 332: Farmall Model B
Date: 1939 Fuel: Distillate   HP: 14 Drawbar, 16 Belt

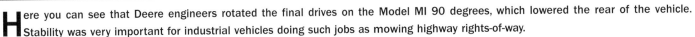

Here you can see that Deere engineers rotated the final drives on the Model MI 90 degrees, which lowered the rear of the vehicle. Stability was very important for industrial vehicles doing such jobs as mowing highway rights-of-way.

Continued from page 55

"Why does the water circulate up in a thermosiphon system? That was a large part of my thesis. You'll find textbooks which say that because of temperature differential throughout the system, whether it's in the block, up around the head, or the top tank, or the bottom tank, or going through the manifold. These differentials in temperatures cause differences in densities. If water is heated, it becomes less dense. So you can reason that this very hot water becomes less dense and will rise to the top, and the more dense water will fall through the core of the radiator, cool, and become denser. Hence, circulation.

"Well, that's the popular notion. When I got into temperature measurement, I discovered that the mean temperature differential was actually getting smaller and smaller as the power increased from 1 horsepower to 20 horsepower. This

temperature differential was supposedly causing circulation. Actually, the temperature differential decreased. From a 1-horsepower output to a 20-horsepower output, the power is increasing 20 times, but the mean temperature differential between the block and the radiator was diminishing. That would suggest that if this hypothesis is true, the flow would diminish if the temperature differential diminished. But the truth of the matter is that the water flow increased drastically as the power went up—like seven or eight times. Here's the temperature differential going down, and yet the water flow is going up—the two curves going the opposite directions. It disproved much of this theory that had been advanced as to why water circulated in a thermosiphon system.

"Okay, what does cause the flow, if it's not the density differential? Well, what happens is a very simple concept. The heat generated in the combustion chamber raises the water to

MINNEAPOLIS-MOLINE MODEL RTU: 1939-1954

A n optional cab was the most novel and exciting design feature of the Minneapolis-Moline (MM) Model RTU. In fact, the Model RTU was the first row-crop tractor available with a factory cab. What made this model even more interesting was the full line of mounted equipment designed to fit around the cab. But, like the famous MM UDLX, the cab concept was about four decades ahead of its time and relatively few Model RTUs were sold with the cab option.

The Model R tractors were the smallest of the MM line but featured the same well-built, long-lived, company-built engine. The Type EE engine was a vertical four-cylinder with a 3- 5/8x4-inch bore and stroke with 165-ci displacement and was rated at 1,400 rpm. An interesting design feature of this engine was the valve positioned horizontally in the block over the piston. The 4/1 transmission allowed working and road speeds of 2-7/16 to 12-1/3 miles per hour.

A starter and lights were optional on early Model RTU tractors. On later models, standard equipment included a Flote-Ride Seat and a six-volt electrical system with starter, generator, battery, instrument panel light, two headlights, and a rearview light. Also available as an option on later models was the three-point "Hitchor" system. Additional options consisted of a hydraulic power lift, 560-rpm PTO, wheel weights, red taillight, muffler extension, and bug screen. A low-compression head was also available for those who wanted to burn the cheaper tractor fuel.

The Model R advertising literature of the late 1940s or early 1950s reflected that the engine rpm was upped to 1,500 and the compression ratio increased. These new models also featured MM's Quick-On-Quick-Off system for mounted implements.

The Model RTU weighed 4,135 pounds, considerably heavier than many of its competitors. It also came with a heftier price tag of about $1,800.

Nebraska Test 341: MM Model RTU

Date: 1940 Fuel: Gasoline   HP: 20 Drawbar, 23 Belt

Nebraska Test 468: MM Model RTU

Date: 1951 Fuel: Gasoline   HP: 23 Drawbar, 23 Belt

Even though this Model MI is wearing Deere's agricultural colors, this front view shows the Industrial front axle, which lowers the front of the vehicle equal with the rear.

This view of the Model M shows the off-center arrangement of the tractor, which provides better visibility for the operator while working row crop. It also provides an interesting comparison to the Industrial Model's front axle.

OLIVER 60: 1940-1948

The Model 60 tractors were a departure in name and styling from the previous Oliver Hart-Parr lineup. The "Hart-Parr" was dropped from the name and the utilitarian, no-frills, look was replaced with sleek new tinwork featuring distinctive louvered engine side panels along with the yellow grille.

The Model 60 was the "baby" of the three new tractors. Its horsepower was generated by an Oliver-Waukesha four-cylinder engine with 3-5/16x3-1/2-inch bore and stroke rated at 1,500 rpm. It displaced 120ci. Introduced as a tricycle or wide-adjustable front axle row-crop model, it was followed in 1942 by the Model 60 standard and industrial models. The 4/1 transmission provided advertised travel of 2-9/16, 3-7/16, 4-9/16, and 6-1/8 miles per hour on either steel wheels or rubber tires. Oliver was one of the first, perhaps *the* first, tractor manufacturer to offer independent PTO.

Without wheel weights or added ballast, the Model 60 tipped the scales at 2,450 pounds. Some Model 60s were manufactured for Cockshutt with appropriate tinwork, paint, and badges. It should be noted that the Cockshutt vehicles did not have the independent PTO.

Approximately 25,130 Model 60s (all variants) were manufactured at the Oliver Farm Equipment Company's Charles City, Iowa, facility.

> **Nebraska Test 375: Oliver 60**
> **Date: 1941 Fuel: Gasoline   HP: 16 Drawbar, 18 Belt**

boiling temperature, and it's generating bubbles. The bubbles are rising rapidly up the water manifold into the top tank. Of course everything has to be flowing upward. Those bubbles are inducing the flow by their contact with water. So, it's nothing but a percolator. Of course the more heat you pump into the cylinder heads the more bubbles you generate, and the bigger the bubbles are the more they are inducing the flow.

"Nordenson didn't buy density differential, and one of the things that was funny to me is that I was able to support the boss' conclusion. If you can do that it helps."

Basic Model M tractors hit the market at about $1,300 to $1,450, depending on the model. The Crawler was understandably higher, and it sold for approximately $2,150.

The approximate weights were as follows: Model M, 2,650 pounds; Model MT, 2,900 pounds; Model MI, 2,950 pounds; and the Model MC, 3,950 pounds.

Model H production ended in 1947, and the Model M was replaced by the Model 40 in 1953. Approximately 145,707 copies of these two Deere products were rolled off the assembly lines to replace horses and mules on the nation's small farms. If one tractor replaced only a single team, that meant 291,414 animals were retired and 1,457,070 acres of land became available for other agricultural uses, based on 5 acres of land to support 1 horse.

Chapter 3

TARGETING THE SINGLE-TEAM FARMS

Models Y, 62, L, LA

Time and again, the tractor business proved a slippery road for tractor manufacturers, including Deere & Company. In 1918, just two years after buying its way into the market by purchasing the Waterloo Boy factory, the viability of Deere's tractor program was in question.

In 1920, the bottom dropped out of the national economy. Agribusiness and farm implement companies were especially hard hit. Dozens of firms were liquidated, and many others fell into receivership.

For many, though, the coup de grace came in January 1921, when Henry Ford fired the opening shot of the "tractor wars" by reducing the price of a Fordson from $785 to $620. International Harvester followed suit in March by dropping the prices on its tractors. One year later, in January 1922, Ford dropped the price of a Fordson to $395, a price so low that scores of companies couldn't compete. Even big General Motors swallowed hard and bowed out of the tractor business in 1922, after suffering a $33 million loss.

By this time Deere was on the ropes and almost out of the tractor game. In 1920, the company sold 5,045 Model N Waterloo Boy tractors. Tractor sales in 1921 registered a mere 79 units, even though, in response to the price slashing that Ford had started, Deere had dropped the price of the Waterloo Boy from $1,150 to $890. The lack of sales and profits forced Deere to lay off employees and cut salaries throughout the organization. There was only one saving grace to the tractor program, and that was research and development. Time and again, R & D not only kept Deere in the arena, but ultimately allowed the company to catapult to number one.

Ongoing product research and development aimed at improving tractor design resulted in the famous Model D, which revitalized Deere & Company's tractor program. Events proved that the 1924 Model D was the right product at the right time, and it was Leon Clausen who was responsible for launching it, despite the fact that some of Deere's management wanted to scrap the entire endeavor.

Deere didn't have much time to relish the D's success, for a few years later the "slippery road" scenario repeated itself. In 1929, the

Only 78 or 79 copies of the Model 62 were produced, and few have survived, making it a very collectable John Deere product. The Model 62 was designed and built at the John Deere Wagon Works in Moline, Illinois.

FORD-FERGUSON 9N & 2N
1939-1947

Henry Ford's desire to build tractors to lessen the hard labor of farming didn't stop in 1928 when he withdrew the Fordson from U.S. production. He continued to build Fordson tractors in Ireland and England, some of which were imported into the United States. On the homefront, Henry's "dream" suffered through a decade of domestic inactivity—except for the experimental tractors that were being developed in a small building close to Ford's Fair Lane home. These experimental tractors ranged from V-8-powered Allis-Chalmers clones to ugly three-wheelers that resembled a junkyard accident more than they did a tractor.

Then Harry Ferguson showed up at Fair Lane with his Ferguson-Brown tractor and hydraulic three-point hitch system. Ford liked what he saw, shook hands with Ferguson, and by 1947 there were 297,129 copies of the little gray 9N and 2N Ford-Ferguson tractors plowing, planting, and cultivating from coast to coast—and dominating the small-tractor market. Remember the rule of thumb that one horse could plow one acre of ground a day? This little tractor could plow an acre an hour!

Two factors made this a dominating — as well as revolutionary — tractor. Ford's manufacturing facilities and very deep pockets kept the price low enough for even the little guy to afford. Plus, both the 9N and 2N featured the three-point hitch and hydraulic system that Ferguson had worked 22 years to develop. Oh, yes—Ferguson's ability to "sell you the birds out of the trees" ensured that a successful national distribution system was quickly put into place.

Powered by one-half of a Ford V-8, the vertical four-cylinder L-head had a 3-3/16x3- 3/4-inch bore and stroke, which displaced 119-ci. It was rated at 2,000 rpm. A 3/1 transmission gave forward travel of 2-1/2, 3-1/4, and 7-7/16 miles per hour.

During the war years, some of the little Fords rolled on steel wheels and were without the normally standard electric starter. Other standard equipment included a generator, battery, PTO, and rubber tires. Headlights were an option. It is likely that more implements and aftermarket products were designed and marketed for the 9N, 2N, and 8N than for any other tractor ever marketed. These implements and products ranged from a jack stand to a road grader conversion, with hundreds of items in between. Records show that between 1939 and 1946, an average of 2.92 implements were sold per tractor. That's an impressive 867,616 implement sales. In addition, though never offered as strictly an industrial vehicle, the 9N and 2N Moto-Tug versions were very popular on military airfields and aircraft carriers.

The Ford Ferguson's dry weight was 2,410 pounds, with an introductory list price of $585.

> **Nebraska Test 339: Ford-Ferguson 9N & 2N**
>
> **Date: 1940 Fuel: Gasoline HP: 17 Drawbar, 23 Belt**

TOUGH TIMES

Fred Hileman began his career with Deere & Company in 1925 and retired in 1969 as director of service in the marketing division. Hileman recounted two stories that give an indication of just how tough the late 1920s and early 1930s were for Deere.

"I'd been down in Fredrick, Oklahoma, for about two months, and I wanted to come home and get married. At first my boss wouldn't answer my letters, but later he told me the sparrows were making more noise in the plant than the machines. That's how tough it was during the Depression," he said.

Hileman also offered this Christmas tale. "I'd been dropped off at a big sheep operation in Tucson, Arizona, to run that experimental tractor program. Come Christmas I was living with the ranch manager. The ranch manager and his family all went to Phoenix or other places for Christmas, and I was left alone and without an automobile. The ranch had two or three Model T Ford pickups with boxes on the back. I decided that I was not going to stay out there on Christmas, so I picked the one that looked the cleanest and I drove into town and parked in an alley. I had my Christmas dinner before dark and then cranked up the truck and went home.

"I sent the bill into Waterloo with a report on my expenses and Deere wouldn't reimburse me. When I got my first chance to talk to the man in charge of the offices, I told him, 'I never got my money.' He looked at me and said, 'We weren't sure we would make it. We were that close to closing down.' As I recall this was 1933."

So, considering the company's financial woes during these years, budgets were tight. Deere was fortunate enough to have had enough cash reserves when the crash came to weather the storm better than most manufacturers, and to continue its research and development efforts.

stock market crashed, and by the early 1930s the Great Depression was a giant, dark shadow on the financial landscape. The picture was made only darker by the rolling dust storms of the 1930s.

Deere & Company's bottom line for 1931 was a $1 million loss on $27.7 million in sales. For 1932, the loss was $5.7 million on $8.7 million in sales. The year 1933 saw sales rise to $9 million but with a $4.3 million dollar loss. Despite these tough times, management insisted that research and development continue, and this foresight eventually resulted in the highly successful Models A and B tractors, which were introduced in 1935. However, their success wasn't yet established in 1935 when the engineering department was once again asked to develop another tractor to fill a specific niche in the line, which led to the development of the Model Y.

MODEL Y: 1936

The Model Y was a low-budget tractor project that was assigned to the engineering team at the John Deere Wagon Works in Moline, Illinois. Ultimately, this tractor division of the Moline engineering department was dignified with the name Wagon Works Tractor Division, which was again changed in 1943 to the John Deere Moline Tractor Works.

In keeping with the restrictions of an almost nonexistent budget, the Model Y was built from existing Deere parts that were mated to outside vendor components. A Novo vertical two-cylinder gas engine was the first power source, but it was soon replaced by another vertical two-cylinder engine by

Continues on page 70

This unstyled Model **L** was built in 1938, the first year of production. The belt pulley was an optional piece of equipment, but otherwise all of the features on this tractor were standard equipment, including the wheels and magneto.

An unstyled Model **L** and a New Generation 1010 share a collector's shop with a Model 630 that is undergoing restoration. The Model **L** is the smallest of the two-cylinder John Deeres and the Model 1010 is the smallest of the New Generation tractors.

MASSEY-HARRIS PONY MODEL 11: 1947-1954

"One Pony beats two horses" was an easy achievement for Massey-Harris' smallest tractor, the Pony. Between 1947 and 1954, a total of 28,746 units rolled off the assembly line at Massey's Woodstock, Ontario, facility.

The Pony, very popular with small-acreage farmers, featured a line of mounted implements that included a planter, cultivator, low, disk, sickle mower, front blade, loader, and others, which gave the owner the ability to do every job on the small farm.

The standard equipment included an electric starter, rubber tires, muffler, and fenders. Options included a hydraulic lift, mechanical lift, belt pulley, PTO, lights, and wheel weights.

The Continental-built gasoline engine was a vertical four-cylinder with 2-3/8x3- 1/2-inch bore and stroke, which displaced 62-ci. Rated at 1,800 rpm, it could be revved up to 1,990 for belt work. The four-banger was mated to a 3/1 transmission, which provided forward speeds of 2-3/4, 3-1/2, and 7 miles per hour.

The Pony weighed in at about 1,520 pounds and was available in two model options: standard and adjustable front axle. The standard front axle model listed at $838, while the adjustable front axle was $854.

In 1954 and 1955, these vehicles were painted gray, equipped with the Ferguson badge, and sold as part of the Ferguson tractor line. An industrial version of the Pony Model 11 was rolled out as the Model 14. The industrial version differed very little from its agricultural sibling with almost all specs being the same. The Model 14, however, had a hydraulic coupling; at 1,896 pounds weighed a bit more; and carried a higher price tag, $1,073. Only 74 industrial copies were produced from 1951 through 1953.

> **Nebraska Test 401: Massey-Harris Pony Model 11**
> **Date: 1948 Fuel: Gasoline   HP: 10 Drawbar, 11 Belt**

From left to right: A 1940 Model L, serial number 631720 with Hercules engine; a 1941 Model LA with a Deere-built engine; and a 1941 LI. These tractors spend a lot of time in parades, which is why there are rearview mirrors mounted on the steering-wheel pedestal. The mirrors are not original equipment.

INTERNATIONAL HARVESTER FARMALL CUB: 1947-1958

International Harvester's (IH) plan for ridding the remaining small farms of those pesky horses and mules was built around the small, but capable, Farmall Cub. IH printed advertisements that in part, read, "The Farmall Cub is . . . designed and built to do easier, faster, and better, every job ordinarily handled by two or three horse or mules . . ." And the plan worked, especially in the southern states, where it proved ideal for tobacco farming and truck farming.

The Cub was one of several small IH tractors that were produced at the company's Louisville Works in Kentucky. Production began at the facility on April 9, 1947, and 23 months later just over 135,000 small Farmall tractors had rolled off the Louisville production line, with Farmall Cubs accounting for 65,000.

Like the Farmall Models A and B, the Cub featured Culti-Vision, with its offset centerline of the engine and driveline and the seat on the right, which provided the operator a clear view when working row crop.

Due to the 1,600 rpm of the Cub's PTO, if a Cub owner wanted to use PTO-powered equipment, it had to be with an IH product designed and built specifically for the Cub. In addition, the Cub PTO rotated in the opposite direction of "normal" PTOs on other farm tractors. IH provided a full line of implements and attachments for the Cub, ensuring that the Cub owner would also be an implement customer.

The Cub's power was derived from an IH-built gasoline vertical four-cylinder engine with 2-5/8x2-3/4-inch bore and stroke displacing 59.5-ci. The little engine turned at a rated speed of 1,600 rpm and utilized thermosiphon cooling. The Cub engine was the only IH powerplant that didn't use sleeved cylinders. Forward speeds of 2-1/8, 3-1/8, and 6-7/16 miles per hour were provided by the 3/1 transmission.

Two front axle designs were available on the Cub: the 40-5/8-inch nonadjustable, or standard, and the 46-3/8-inch adjustable. The rear tread width was adjustable from 40 to 56 inches.

The standard equipment didn't include a battery, electric starter, or electric lights, although they were available as options. An electric lighting and starting package was also available for magneto-equipped units. The IH Touch Control hydraulic system wasn't quite ready when production began, so the first production tractors were hand-lift only for mounted equipment. By early 1948, the Touch Control system and field installation were available for early-production tractors.

The Cub was a very successful tractor for IH, with just over 203,000 units built from introduction through 1958. Not bad for a tractor that went head-to-head with the Ford 8N, which was introduced in 1948 with several improvements to the engine, transmission, and hydraulic system over the previous 9N and 2N.

After 1958 the original Cub underwent several design changes and remained in the IH line until 1979. The Cub was definitely a lightweight at 1,430 pounds. The price in 1954 was $905.

Nebraska Test 386: Farmall Cub

Date: 1947   Fuel: Gasoline   HP: 8 Drawbar, 9 Belt

A welcome feature of John Deere's two-cylinder design was simplicity, at a time when farmers had to learn the new skills required to maintain and repair tractors. Farmers often relied on the local blacksmith to keep horsepower, such as this team of Belgian horses and a 1941 Model LA, operating smoothly.

Continued from page 66

Hercules. The Ford Model A's transmission and steering gear were integrated into the Model Y, which rode on wheels from a John Deere manure spreader.

Depending on the source, 24 or 26 Model Ys made. All were hand-built, and all were believed to have been recalled by the factory and destroyed—with the possible exception of one.

The 3x4-inch bore and stroke engine displaced 56.48-ci, and although it was never tested at Nebraska, it probably peaked at about eight drawbar horsepower.

The suggested retail price was set at $532.50. A Garden Cultivator and Garden Planter were implements designed for the Model Y.

Model 62: 1937

In early 1937, the Model Y was redesigned and reclassified as the Model 62. In reality, this tractor served more as

a prototype for the Model L than as a consumer product. Depending on the source of information, there were 78 or 79 copies of the Model 62 produced before its metamorphosis into the Model L. Model 62 serial numbers began with 621000.

The Model 62 was an unstyled tractor, but with a real beauty mark on the casting below the radiator. The large JD in the casting makes it easily distinguishable from the unstyled Model L. The JD is also found on the back of the differential casting.

The Model 62's offset design, which placed the engine and drivetrain off-center left and the operator's seat off-center right, allowed for exceptional visibility for working a single-row crop.

Powered by a 3x4-inch bore and stroke Hercules NXA vertical gasoline engine that displaced 56.48-ci, the Model 62 also featured the standard Deere thermosiphon cooling system.

SEAT FOR ONE

The Model Y's seat was padded with a backrest, an obvious move to improve operator comfort, but it didn't survive the transition to the Model 62 or subsequent Model L model. For whatever reason, most likely economics, the Model L seat was a continuation of the metal implement seat that was spawned somewhere in antiquity.

Jack Cade left the Dayton-Dick Company, builders of Leader Tractors, and joined the Deere & Company engineering team in 1920. Cade had also worked closely with Charlie Hart of the Hart-Parr Company in Charles City, Iowa.

Cade's paper, *Reminiscences of 40 Years With John Deere*, gives this observation on the rather Spartan operator seats on early tractors. "There was an article in an early *Farm Implement News* that described how these implement seats were made. The designer took a common metal wash basin and threw it up in the air, shot it full of holes with a shotgun, and then ran over it with a tractor. The seat thus formed was fastened to the implement with a bolt through the center. The bolt soon pulled through the metal, so he added a washer and larger bolt. As breakage continued, he kept adding a larger washer under the preceding one until finally you just rode on a stack of washers."

William Hewitt was president and CEO of Deere from 1955 to 1964, chairman and CEO 1964 to 1982, and son-in-law of Charles Deere Wiman. He spoke of the engineering specification for the iron seats on the early tractors. "We designed tractor seats by having Ol' Sam sit in some plaster of Paris. He had the biggest butt in the factory, and his form became the shape of the tractor seat! These were known as saddle seats.

"A piece of extremely heavy sheet metal was pressed, more or less in this form. There was no cushion at all. The seat had perforations for ventilation which read, 'Deere & Company.' In those days I used to say, 'Our name really makes an impression on the operators!' "

Never tested at Nebraska, the Model 62 probably had the same seven or eight drawbar horsepower as the unstyled Model L.

MODEL L: 1937–1946

The Model L rolled off the assembly line in late 1937 sporting the best features of its two predecessors, the Y and 62. It was Deere's smallest farm tractor and cost-cutting measures were incorporated to enhance the bottom line. Gone was the "JD" on the front shield below the radiator. The fenders were changed to a clamshell design to save material, and the wheels were made of steel rather than cast-iron. Incidentally, there is no indication that the Model Y, Model 62, or any of the Model L tractors were ever produced with anything other than rubber tires.

Starting with serial number 629000 on the early styled Model L, the transmission gear speeds changed. Though the transmission was still a 3/1, it now boasted speeds of 2, 3-1/2, and 6-1/2 miles per hour. This change reflected the discontinuation of the Spicer tranny and the introduction of the Deere-built design. Although very similar, the gear shift lever on the Deere tranny was on the side of the case, while the Spicer was located on the top.

A full line of mounted or pull-type equipment was available, but the Model L never offered a mechanical or hydraulic lift. The mounted equipment designed for the Models L and LA included one- and two-row planters with fertilizer attachment; one-bottom plow; middlebreaker; one- and two-row cultivators; sicklebar mower; side-delivery rake; and four-row vegetable planter. Available pull-type implements were moldboard and disk plows; tillers; spike-tooth and spring-tooth harrows; rotary hoe; corn planter; grain drill; mower; rake; hay loader; and manure spreader.

ALLIS-CHALMERS MODEL G 1948-1955

From a modern perspective it is difficult to appreciate the feelings on both sides of the horse-versus-tractor drama that was played out during the first half of the twentieth century.

This quote from Walter F. Peterson's work, *An Industrial Heritage: Allis-Chalmers Corporation*, helps put it in perspective: "Although the horse has always been loved by some as an intelligent and handsome animal, the tractor division of Allis-Chalmers (AC) was dedicated to a reduction in the number of horses in the country, because each one meant a potential tractor sale. The spirit of the sales department is evident in a statement attributed to Bill Roberts that he hoped to live to see the day when children would have to go to a zoo to see a horse."

Allis-Chalmers designed the Model G as part of the company's effort to accomplish this goal. Departing from the standard tractor design with the engine up front over the steering axle and drive wheels at the rear, the Model G put the engine over the rear axle for traction while leaving the front of the vehicle open for unrestricted operator visibility. The Model G was unmatched for close-tolerance row-crop work.

Although not a major threat to the horse population, the Model G did sell almost 30,000 copies during its lifetime. The entire production came from AC's Gadsden, Alabama, facility. Rather than tool up to build an engine small enough for the Model G, AC outsourced a four-cylinder powerplant from Continental. The engine displaced a mere 62-ci from a 2-3/8x3-1/2-inch bore and stroke. It was rated at 1,800 rpm and mated to a 4/1 transmission. A special creeper low gear allowed the operator to slow to 3/4 miles per hour for precise cultivation of specialty crops.

The front and rear tread width could be adjusted from 36 to 64 inches. The Model G was a petite 1,285 pounds with a 1949 list price of $760. Options included a belt pulley and hydraulic lift.

> **Nebraska Test 398: Allis-Chalmers Model G**
> **Date: 1948 Fuel: Gasoline HP: 9 Drawbar, 10 Belt**

The Model L Series tractors departed from previous models by utilizing a foot clutch instead of the traditional hand clutch. Individual rear-wheel brakes allowed the tractor to turn in a 7-foot radius. The Model L never offered PTO, but a belt pulley was available as an option.

A base weight of 2,180 pounds was listed at the Nebraska tests for the early-styled Model L, and in 1940 the price tag was $477.

> **Nebraska Test 313: Model L**
> **Date: 1938 Fuel: Gasoline HP: 9 Drawbar, 10 Belt**

Unstyled Model L: 1937–1938

Serial numbers 621079 through 622580 indicate a vehicle with the 3.00x4.00-inch Hercules NXA vertical gasoline engine, of which 1,502 were produced. A small number were

The serial number on this 1944 Industrial Model L is IL 50943. The electric starter and lights were optional.

painted industrial yellow and served in areas other than agricultural service.

Model L Early Styled: 1938–1941

In 1938, the Model L received a new look that kept up with the Dreyfuss styling of the Models A, B, and D tractors. Early-styled Model L production, using the Hercules NXB engine, carried serial numbers 625000 through 634840.

The styling was achieved primarily by new tinwork on the hood and grille. A taller front axle and larger rear tires added 3 inches of clearance, thus transforming the Model L into a Hi-Clearance model. All 3,263 of the Model L Hi-Clearance models used Hercules engines.

The Model LA could route 14 horsepower though the pulley, which was optional equipment. That's enough power for buzz-sawing firewood, powering a hammer mill, or any of a dozen other light chores around the farm.

AVERY MODEL A: 1943-1950

B. F. Avery & Sons Company of Louisville, Kentucky, can trace its history back over 125 years, placing it among the country's oldest agricultural equipment manufacturers. Its products were sold worldwide, and for many years the export markets played an important role in the company's growth.

In 1939 the Avery firm signed a contract that gave Montgomery Ward & Company distribution rights for Avery farm implements in territories not served by Avery branches and dealers. As of 1948, Avery maintained company branch houses in Dallas, Texas, and Memphis, Tennessee.

Also in 1939, Avery entered the power farming trend by building a line of tractor-drawn implements and contracting with an outside firm to build a tractor from Avery's design. By 1942, Avery was ready to manufacture its own tractor, and the Avery Model A was introduced to the world.

Avery's line of tractors consisted of small vehicles aimed at the row-crop farms of the South, especially tobacco farms. The early Model A used a four-cylinder Hercules engine with a 3-1/8x4-inch bore and stroke. Later models switched to a Hercules IXB-3 with a 3-1/4x4-inch bore and stroke design displacing 133-ci. The Model A could handle two 12-inch bottom plows; it had a single front wheel and adjustable rear wheels.

Along with the Model A comes a complete line of Tru-Draft equipment for the tractor. The principle of Tru-Draft, as applied to the Avery implements, meant they were hitched "from center-of-load to center-of-power," as stated in company advertising. By attaching in this manner, the implements were allowed to float free of the tractor, and a minimum amount of power and fuel was required to pull the implements in their natural line of draft.

The Model A sold approximately 20,114 copies. It was never tested at Nebraska.

AVERY MODEL V: 1946-1952

In 1946 Avery introduced the Model V, which stayed in the line until 1952, with total production reaching 7,267 units. This tractor was a one-plow model with a ZXB-3 Hercules engine and a 3/1 transmission. The four-cylinder engine had a 2-5/8x3-inch bore and stroke displacing 64-ci.

This was a standard-tread tractor with a channel iron frame, and a front cross-member for attaching the Tru-Draft implements. The Model V was never tested at Nebraska.

A Deere-designed, Hercules-built, NXA vertical L-head two-cylinder gasoline engine was the powerplant. With 3-1/4x4-inch bore and stroke, it displaced 66-ci and turned at a rated rpm of 1,550. The 3/1 transmission had forward speeds of 2-1/2, 3-3/4, and 6 miles per hour.

Both the early-styled and late-styled styled Model Ls continued in the Deere General Purpose line until 1946.

Styled versions of the Model L racked up a total production number of 11,225.

Model L Late-Styled: 1941–1946

These vehicles, serial numbers 640000 through 642038, were fitted with a 3-1/4x4-inch John Deere-built vertical gasoline engine. An electric starter and lights became an option with this line as well.

AVERY/MINNEAPOLIS-MOLINE MODEL R: 1950-1951

On March 1, 1951, B. F. Avery merged with the Minneapolis-Moline (MM) firm, which became the surviving company. MM was the firm that retained its name and control of the new company. The Model R could be called a transitional tractor because it was introduced in 1950, just a year prior to the merger. In 1952, the Model R became the MM Model BF, and was decked out in a Prairie Gold paint scheme instead of Avery Red.

While the Model A and Model V had a 3/1 transmission, the Model R came with a 4/1. After the Model R designation changed to BF, production continued until 1953, with a total of 2,078 vehicles manufactured.

MODEL BF: 1952-1953

In 1953, the Model BF became available in three different front axle configurations: BFS, which was a single-front-wheel configuration (production was 47 tractors); BFD, a dual-front-wheel tricycle (production was 358 tractors); and BFW, a wide-adjustable front axle (production was 1,034). The BFW front axle was adjustable from 52 inches to 72 inches. All models had an adjustable rear tread from 52 inches to 76 inches in 4-inch steps. Special rear tires and a modified front axle transformed the BF into the BFH Hi-Crop model, which had 27-1/2-inch crop clearance. The production numbers were 150 copies.

All models used a four-cylinder IXB3SL 133-ci Hercules engine with a 3-1/4x4-inch bore and stroke with variable governing from 1,200 to 1,800 rpm. A 4/1 transmission allowed forward travel of 1-5/8 to 13 miles per hour.

After the merger, until 1952, these tractors carried both the MM and Avery badge.

> **Nebraska Test 469: Model BF**
>
> **Date: 1951 Fuel: Gasoline   HP: 24 Drawbar, 27 Belt**

MM MODEL BG: 1953-1955

The Model BG, 1953 to 1955, used the 1X3SL Hercules engine with 133-ci mated to a 4/1 transmission. The BG was a one-row outfit, and the offset steering design gave excellent visibility. An even 1,200 copies were produced. With the Model BG, the Avery name disappeared from the BG and BF models. The BG was never tested at Nebraska.

Model LI: 1941–1946

The LI was an industrial model of the Model L. Official production of the LI began in 1941. However, some earlier-production tractors were considered industrial models.

The Deere-built engine was standard in the Model LI from 1941 to 1946. The Model L styled tractors that were dubbed industrial before 1941 were fitted with the Hercules engine. The LI was not tested at Nebraska.

Model LA: 1941–1946

The Model LA differs from the Model L mainly under the hood. The Deere-built vertical two-cylinder engine had a 3-1/2x4-inch bore and stroke engine, which rated at 1,850 rpm and displaced 77-ci. That's 1/4-inch greater bore, a 300-rpm increase, and 11 more cubic inches than the Model L. It all added up to a more than 40 percent increase in power, and the LA churned out as much horsepower as the Model H. Options included an electric

starter, lights, generator and battery, adjustable front axle, PTO, front and rear weights, and belt pulley.

The Model LA was assigned a new block of serial numbers that started with 1001 and probably ended with 13475, meaning production totals equaled about 12,475 copies. As far as an industrial version of the Model LA, an unknown number were produced.

Nebraska test information places the LA's base weight at 2,285 pounds. When the LA was phased out in 1946, the price was only $577.

Nebraska Test 373: Model LA
Date: 1941 Fuel: Gasoline   HP: 13 Drawbar, 14 Belt

DEERE: AN INDUSTRY LEADER

By the mid-1940s, Deere & Company's line included the Model D and Model G as the big tractors; the Model A, Model B, and Model H as midline power; and the small-tractor end was covered by the Model L and Model LA. Any farm, no matter how large or how small, could find a John Deere tractor of the right size to replace several teams of horses, or a single team. While Deere had grown into an industry leader, the work-animal population had fallen, to 11,629,000—less than half of the high mark of 26,723,000, recorded in 1918—the year Deere purchased the Waterloo Boy plant.

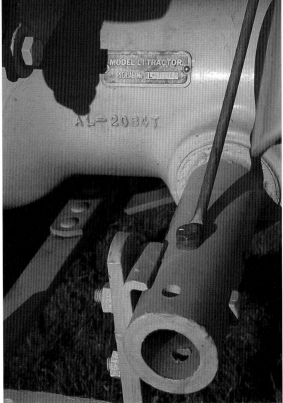

Left, right, and above

Three different strengths of pipe were used in constructing frames for the Model 62 and Model Ls. Shown left to right, the thinnest wall pipe on a Model 62, the solid pipe frame on a Model LA, and the heavy wall pipe on the Model LI.

Chapter 4

ROUNDING UP THE LAST HAY BURNERS

Models 40 and 50

By the close of the 1940s, the design of the tractor had pretty well been standardized into the four-wheel, front-engine, rear-wheel-drive configuration. Engineering advances in metallurgy, fuels, and manufacturing processes had allowed the tractor to evolve from the giant 10-ton units of the first and second decades of the twentieth century to the 1-ton row-crop tractors that replaced the final teams of horses on even the smallest farms.

79

Previous pages

This 1954 Model 40 Utility probably doesn't look forward to sundown now the way it did in its working days. But a lighting package with front and rear lights meant the working day could be stretched far past sundown. The split grille was adopted at serial number 63120, so this vehicle was built prior to that time.

The late 1940s saw the revisiting of the trend toward bigger—and better. Bigger meant more horsepower from the same smaller-sized tractors. Better meant easier-to-use, trouble-free, and handy tractors. After World War II, farmers began expecting more power and more operator conveniences.

From the Model D of 1923 to the Model R of 1949, it could be argued that the Deere line had evolved from a mostly trial-and-error process spawned by some internal or external crisis. But through good times and bad, Deere had established itself as a major competitor in the tractor game through its innovative research and results.

As the world entered the 1950s, the time had arrived to design a line of tractors that would serve the needs of any farm. This resulted in the introduction of John Deere's first Numbered Series, which ranged from the Model 40 with 21 drawbar horsepower to the Model 80, which delivered 60 drawbar horsepower.

MODEL 40 SERIES: 1953–1955

The smallest of the numbered Deere tractors (excluding the Model 62) was the Model 40, which the company brought online in 1953. Approximately 49,000 copies of the Model 40 Series were produced during its three-year lifetime.

Deere viewed the new series as totally new tractors, announcing, "The Model 40 Series tractors are new from stem to stern." Granted, they did have a long list of truly new features. However, a very pronounced shadow of the Model M lurked beneath new tinwork. And, like the Model M, the 40 Series was produced at Deere's Dubuque, Iowa, facility.

A cast-iron front axle under this 1953 Model 40 Tricycle allows the tread width to be adjusted from 48 to 80 inches. Fitted with 34-inch rear wheels, it allowed approximately 21 inches of crop clearance under the rear axle.

FORD MODEL 8N: 1948-1952

In 1945, at the age of 82, Henry Ford called it quits, reluctantly handing the reins of power to his grandson, 28-year-old Henry II.

The decision that most affected the production of tractors occurred in late 1946. Henry II informed Harry Ferguson that his handshake agreement with his grandfather would no longer be honored. Ford would continue to supply Ferguson's distribution company with tractors only until mid-1947.

Ford planned to introduce a new tractor, to be known as the Ford 8N. The new tractor would employ the Ferguson three-point hydraulic system with little modification, no apology, and no license or royalty fees. Furthermore, Ford intended to establish its own marketing network and its own line of implements. This was accomplished under the newly formed Dearborn Motors.

Available beginning in July 1947, sales of the new 8N were strong, and by the end of the year almost 38,000 copies were produced. At the conclusion of production in 1952, a remarkable 524,076 8Ns could be found on large and small farms across America.

The size and appearance of the 8N closely resembled the Ford-Ferguson 9N and 2N, with two notable exceptions: The tinwork, fenders, hood, grille, and wheels were a lighter shade of gray, while the engine, transmission housing, differential, and front and rear hubs were bright red, which resulted in the nickname "red belly."

There were some innovative nuts-and-bolts changes to the tractor. Manufacturers were discovering that farmers wanted more than a three-speed transmission to better match ground speed to field work. Thus, the 8N was introduced with a four-speed tranny instead of the previous three-speed.

The Ford-built vertical four-cylinder engine retained the same 3-3/16x3-3/4-inch bore and stroke, which yielded 119.7-ci. For drawbar work, it was rated at 1,400 rpm; for belt work it was upped to 2,000 rpm. Initially it had the same 6:1 compression ratio as the 9N, but it was soon changed to 6.37:1 and then 6.5:1.

Although it was still basically a vintage Ferguson design, the hydraulic system on the Model 8N received some design improvements. A position-control setting was added, which allowed the operator to override the automatic depth control. Perhaps the most appreciated change for the tractor operator was positioning both brake pedals on the right side of the tractor. Now the clutch and left brake could easily be engaged at the same time. Finally, running boards were provided as standard equipment.

The normal tread width was 64-3/4 inches. However, both the front and rear tread could be adjusted from 48 to 76 inches in 4-inch increments. The tractor weighed 2,410 pounds and carried a 1952 price tag of $1,200.

It is doubtful that any other tractor ever had so many different implements and attachments designed for it by the company and a bevy of aftermarket firms. Eventually, this line of implements grew to approximately 400 items.

Nebraska Test 385: Ford Model 8N
Date: 1947 Fuel: Gasoline   HP: 17 Drawbar, 21 Belt
Nebraska Test 393: Ford Model 8N
Date: 1948 Fuel: Gasoline   HP: 21 Drawbar, 25 Belt
Nebraska Test 443: Ford Model 8N
Date: 1950 Fuel: Gasoline   HP: 21 Drawbar, 26 Belt

A shot across the bow of a Model 40 Tricycle accents the Model 40 Utility's lower stance. This 1954 Model 40 Utility is 1 of 5,208 copies made at Deere & Company's Dubuque, Iowa, factory.

The vertical two-cylinder engine, for all models, was vintage Model M tweaked just a trifle. The 4x4-inch bore and stroke remained the same, but the rpm was increased from 1,650 to 1,850, and the compression ratio went from 6.0:1 to 6.5:1. Of course, the 100-ci remained the same. These features combined increased the horsepower approximately 15 percent over the Model M engine. The engine was available as an all-fuel or gasoline powerplant. The compression ratio of the all-fuel engine was 4.7:1.

On wheeled models, the 4/1 transmission gave forward travel of 1-5/8, 3-1/8, 4-1/4, and 12 miles per hour. Reverse

The most popular version of the Model 40 was the Tricycle. This 1953 model was 1 of 17,906.

FERGUSON TO-20: 1948-1951

When Ford and Ferguson split the sheets, both were immediately faced with a major problem: Ford had a new tractor but no implements, and Ferguson had an extensive line of implements but no tractor.

Both solved their individual problems rather quickly.

Almost immediately, Ferguson began to import the Ferguson TE-20 from the production facility in the United Kingdom. Perhaps seeing the writing on the wall, Ferguson had begun manufacturing the TE-20 in 1946. However, production numbers were not sufficient to provide a long-term fix.

One option was for Ferguson to build or buy his own tractor production facility in the United States. After investigating several options, Ferguson located and purchased a facility in Detroit, Michigan, from which the first U.S.-built Ferguson TO-20 rolled off the assembly line in 1948.

The same Continental Z-120 four-cylinder gasoline engine that powered the TE-20 was also used to power the American-built TO-20. The Continental engine was an I-head with a 3-3/16x3-3/4-inch bore and stroke rated at 1,750 rpm. Interestingly enough, it is the same bore and stroke as the Ford 8N engine, displacing the same 119.7-ci. As with the 8N, power was channeled through a 4/1 transmission, which allowed the TO-20 to roll along at about 3, 4, 5-1/2, and 11-1/2 miles per hour.

In Ferguson's designation system, "T" was for tractor, "E" for manufactured in England, and "O" for manufactured overseas—from a U.K. reference point. Between 1946 and 1956 over a half-million "Grey Fergies" were built in England. The U.S. production of the TO-20 was a more modest 60,000 copies.

Without added weights or ballast, the TO-20 weighed 2,760 pounds and was perhaps a little more pricey than the 8N, with one source listing the TO-20 at $1,570.

Like the 9N and 2N, the Ferguson was painted all gray, or grey, and from a distance it's difficult to distinguish between the two. And, like Dearborn Motor's 8N, a large number of implements and attachments were available for the Ferguson tractors.

Nebraska Test 392: Ferguson TO-20

Date: 1948 Fuel: Gasoline HP: 20 Drawbar, 25 Belt

---

speed was increased from 1.6 to 2.6 miles per hour. The Crawler's 4/1 tranny speeds were 7/8, 2-1/4, 3, and 5-1/4 miles per hour forward and 1-3/4 miles per hour in reverse.

The old saying, "If you can't beat 'em, join 'em," finally included John Deere when it came to competing with the Ford-Ferguson three-point hitch system. One of the most important features of the Model 40 Series was the new hydraulic system with an industry-standard three-point hitch. The system was live with the Dual Touch-O-Matic control system, coupled to the new Load-and-Depth Control feature. The Dual Touch-O-Matic allowed the operator to independently control either side of the split rockshaft, which made it possible to raise or lower either side independently. Load-and-Depth Control regulated the working depth of mounted equipment, a feature that ensured that on uneven or varying soil conditions, the planting depth or cultivating depth would remain constant.

Specially designed for the Model 40 Series were 23 rear-mounted three-point Quik-Tatch implements and

Is something missing on the dash of this Model 40 Tricycle? Not really. The two empty holes are there if needed, though. The one on the tractor's left is for the fuel switch for an all-fuel engine, and the one on the right is for the radiator shutter control.

Power-adjust rear wheels for the Model 40s were available as an option. Here they are seen with the proper paint scheme—bright silver rims and rails—on a Model 40 Utility.

four midmounted tools. Optional accessories included an hour meter, full front and rear lighting equipment, belt pulley, wheel weight for front or rear, fenders, radiator shutter, and cigarette lighter. One of the most appreciated improvements was a new padded seat that eventually evolved into the deluxe seat featured on the New Generation tractors.

The Model 40 departed from the traditional nomenclature when referring to the Tricycle tractor, which was usually applied to tractors with a narrow front axle with close-together dual wheels or a single front wheel. In the case of the Model 40, the Model 40T included the conventional dual-

wheel and single-front-wheel options, as well as two wide-adjustable front axles.

Model 40S Standard: 1953–1955

Viewed as a two-plow general-purpose tractor, the Standard version of the Model 40 was popular with vegetable growers who planted and cultivated one row at a time. The standard rear-wheel tread was adjustable from 38-3/4 to 55-3/4 inches, while the front tread was adjustable from 40 to 55 inches. The optional power-adjusted rear wheels provided tread width from 39-1/8 to 66-3/8 inches.

FERGUSON TO-30: 1951-1954

The "horsepower race" applied to small tractors as well as large models, and this race caused Ferguson to discontinue the TO-20 and introduce the slightly more powerful TO-30 in 1951.

Ferguson continued using a Continental engine, this time the Z-129, which was an I-head vertical four-cylinder with a 3-1/4x3-7/8-inch bore and stroke that produced 129-ci. It was rated at 1,750 rpm, the same as the TO-20. Essentially it was a bored out TO-20 powerplant that routed the two extra horses through a 4/1 tranny, with specs very similar to the TO-20.

The shipping weight was 2,843 pounds, with a $1,785 price tag. Approximately 80,000 units were produced at the Detroit factory.

Nebraska Test 466: Ferguson TO-30
Date: 1951 Fuel: Gasoline   HP: 24 Drawbar, 29 Belt

Since it left the factory with agricultural green and yellow paint, this 1953 Model 40 Crawler should feel right at home on a western Kansas farm. This three-roller unit is serial number 61312.

MASSEY-HARRIS MODEL 16 PACER: 1954-1956

On August 16, 1953, an official announcement confirmed the merger between Harry Ferguson Ltd. and Massey-Harris of Canada. The prospect of bringing Ferguson's tractor line on board with the Ferguson system, royalty free, was a key factor in the merger. The new company was known as Massey-Harris-Ferguson, and for the first several years they maintained separate tractor lines—Massey-Harris and Ferguson.

In 1954, M-H upgraded its Pony and dubbed it the Pacer. Massey chose Continental's vertical four-cylinder gasoline industrial engine with its 2-7/8x3-1/2-inch bore and stroke to power the Pacer. It provided 91-ci with a rated 1,800 rpm. Forward speeds of approximately 2- 7/8, 3-3/4, and 7-3/8 miles per hour were provided by the 3/1 transmission.

Standard equipment was an adjustable wide front axle capable of front-tread width settings from a narrow 38 inches to only 58 inches. With the optional wide-adjustable front axle, the maximum front tread could be stretched to 75-1/2 inches. The rear-tread adjustment was from 38 to 71 inches, depending on tire size.

Some of the more important standard equipment included the Depth-O-Matic hydraulic system, adjustable front axle, deluxe padded seat, starter, battery ignition, and lights. A belt pulley, PTO, and wheel weights were offered as optional equipment.

Even with improved operator comforts, such as a padded seat with back rest, and other standard features, such as a larger engine and hydraulic lift equipment, the Pacer couldn't keep pace with the competition. Approximately 165 units were produced in 1953, and when production ceased in 1955, only about 2,767 Pacers had entered the farm machinery work force.

The price tag on a Pacer was in the $1,300-plus range for the basic vehicle. Different sources listed different weights of 1,980 pounds or 2,299 pounds.

> **Nebraska Test 531: Massey-Harris Model 16 Pacer**
> **Date: 1954 Fuel: Gasoline   HP: 17 Drawbar, 18 Belt**

An agricultural Model 40 Crawler outfitted with a No. 61 dozer was a handy item to have around the farm for building ponds, clearing brush and hedgerows, or for any number of earth-moving jobs.

^AModel 40 Crawler's dash and controls.

steel. Both offered varying tread widths from 48 to 80 inches. The front-axle configurations and options made the Tricycle well suited for two-row planting and cultivating specialty crops, especially narrow-row vegetable farming.

Two rear axle lengths were available—the regular length gave tread width from 48 to 96 inches if the hubs and wheels were reversed. The optional short axle only provided 48 to 88 inches of rear-tread adjustment.

The 40T tipped the scales at 3,000 pounds without weights or ballast, and in 1955 listed at $1,541 for the traditional tricycle; $1,563.75 for the single front wheel; or $1,655.50 for the wide-adjustable front axle, less any horse-trading the dealer and customer could agree upon.

Depending on rear tire size, the 40T provided approximately 21 inches of crop clearance under the rear axle and measured 58-3/4 inches to the top of the hood. The vehicle length was almost 11 feet, or 130-5/8 inches long.

Nebraska Test 503: Model 40T Tricycle
Date: 1953   Fuel: Gasoline   HP: 21 Drawbar, 24 Belt

Model 40U Utility: 1953–1955

What made this model more of a utility tractor than its siblings, given that they were all small, highly maneuverable, and responsive little tractors? Versatility. It could be used for general agricultural tasks. Or, with the orchard muffler laid horizontally to the rear, it served as the Model 40 version of an orchard vehicle. With a coat of yellow industrial or orange highway paint, it became the Industrial Model 40. While some of the other models may have also received yellow or orange paint schemes, the Model 40U was the most likely to receive this honor.

The Model 40U's low stance and wide-adjustable front axle gave it great stability for the additional roles it was asked to fill, such as highway mowing, orchard and vineyard work, or helping on a construction site. The overall length was 10 feet, 5 inches (126 inches), and height to the hood was a mere 50-1/4 inches. The front-axle tread adjustment was 43 to 56 inches, depending on tire size, while the rear tread was adjustable from 40-7/8 to 57-7/8 inches. If the option of power-adjust rear wheel was specified, the maximum tread adjustment was 68-1/2 inches.

The Model 40U's weight was 2,850 pounds, and the Model 40U's 1995 list price was $1,565.

Model 40W Two-Row Utility: 1955 Only

Only 1,758 copies of this model were produced, between January and October 1955. Lower, and therefore more stable,

Weighing in at 2,750 pounds, the Model 40S had an overall length of 114-3/4 inches and stood 55-1/2 inches to the top of the hood. The 1955 base price was $1,521.50.

Nebraska Test 504: Model 40S Standard
Date: 1953 Fuel: Gasoline   HP: 21 Drawbar, 23 Belt
Nebraska Test 546: Model 40S Standard
Date: 1955 Fuel: Tractor Fuel HP: 18 Drawbar, 20 Belt

Model 40T Tricycle: 1953–1955

The Tricycle accounted for the highest number of 40 Series vehicles, with a production total of 17,906. The Tricycle offered three different front-axle configurations—the dual front-wheel tricycle, the single wheel, and the wide adjustable. The wide adjustable was available in either cast-iron or tubular

OLIVER 66: 1949-1954

Oliver tractors were built at Charles City, Iowa, where the tractor plant covered 17 acres under its roof. The entire complex, including a test track, was located on 65 acres. Charles City has the distinction of being home to the first tractor plant in the United States, for it was here that Charles W. Hart and Charles H. Parr began manufacturing tractors in 1902.

Back in 1855, James Oliver purchased part interest in a foundry, which eventually led to the Oliver Chilled Plow Works of South Bend, Indiana; it merged with Hart-Parr and two other machinery companies to form the Oliver Farm Equipment Company. From this merger in 1929 eventually came the famous Model 66, Model 77, and Model 88 tractors of the Oliver Fleetline Series. Eventually several variations of the Model 66 were produced, including the Row Crop, Standard, Orchard, and Industrial.

The engines for the new series have an interesting history as explained by authors T. Herbert Morrell & Jeff Hackett in their work, *Oliver Farm Tractors*:

> Another challenge was determining where to build the engines. There were not enough laborers available in the Charles City area to build 25,000 to 30,000 tractors per year, and also manufacture the engines. The Waukesha Motor Company in Waukesha, Wisconsin, had manufactured the Oliver Model 60 and Model 80 engines and was quite interested in a contract with Oliver to build engines for the new Fleetline tractors.
>
> We worked out an arrangement with McCoy Truck Lines using two trucks, one operating in Iowa and the other in Wisconsin. The Iowa truck transported the engine casting from Oliver's foundry in Charles City to Prairie du Chien, where they were picked up by the Wisconsin truck and taken to Waukesha Motors plant in Waukesha.
>
> On the return trip the Wisconsin truck took a trailer load of engines to Prairie du Chien, where they were picked up by the Iowa truck and taken to the Charles City plant assembly line.

This well-traveled Oliver/Waukesha-built engine for the Model 66 was a four-cylinder vertical I-head with 129-ci from a 3-5/16x3-3/4-inch bore and stroke rated at 1,600 rpm. Compression ratios were carefully chosen for each fuel option— gasoline, kerosene, and diesel—and were 6.75:1, 4.75:1, and 15:1, respectively. This helped obtain maximum power and fuel efficiency from the customer's fuel preference.

Diesel had proved so popular as a tractor fuel that, "By 1954, before the competition caught up to Oliver, Oliver was selling 45 to 50 percent of all diesel agricultural tractors," according to *Oliver Farm Tractors*.

Oliver designed a 6/2 transmission for the Model 66 that had a bottom end of 2-1/2 miles per hour and a top end of 11-3/8 miles per hour for forward travel. Reverse speeds were 2-1/2 and 4-1/2 miles per hour.

With its Ridemaster Seat, Oliver was one of the first tractor manufacturers to provide easier riding. This new level of operator comfort was introduced on the Fleetline tractors in 1949 and provided Oliver owners with one of the best rides in the field. Oliver was also one of the first companies to introduce disc brakes on agricultural tractors. They became available on the Fleetline tractors beginning in 1950 and 1951.

Nebraska test data lists the Model 66 Row-Crop as weighing 3,193 pounds, while the Standard 66 tipped the scales at 2,919 pounds. The Model 66 Row-Crop tractor carried a retail list price of $1,940.

Nebraska Test 412: Oliver 66 Tricycle Row Crop

Date: 1949   Fuel: Gasoline   HP: 21 Drawbar, 24 Belt

Nebraska Test 413: Oliver 66 Standard

Date: 1949   Fuel: Gasoline   HP: 21 Drawbar, 24 Belt

Nebraska Test 467: Oliver 66 Tricycle Row-Crop Diesel

Date: 1951   Fuel: Diesel   HP: 22 Drawbar, 25 Belt

This is the first prototype of the Model 40 Hi-Crop to come out of the Dubuque, Iowa, experimental shop. The vehicle was finished and rolled out for this photograph in April 1954. The building in the background is the experimental prototype shop at the Dubuque facility. *Mike Mack*

than the Model 40 Tricycle, the Model 40W had just 17 inches of clearance under the rear axle. Nevertheless, it was a popular tractor for cultivating row crop with its front-mounted Quik-Tatch cultivator.

The Model 40W weighed 3,000 pounds, the same as the Tricycle 40, and sold for $1,650.

Model 40H Hi-Crop: 1954–1955

This was a relatively low-production tractor, with only 294 copies made during 14 months of production, between August 1954, and October 1955. By utilizing larger tires, longer front-axle spindles, and drop housings on the rear axle, the Hi-Crop stood 67-1/8 inches at the hoodline and provided 32 inches of crop clearance. The tread adjustment for both front and rear axles was 54 to 84 inches, in 6-inch increments. The overall length was 132 inches, or exactly 11 feet.

Under-the-axle clearance is the objective of a Hi-Crop tractor, and this view shows a lot of daylight between the ground and the axle housings—a full 32 inches. Production began on the 40 Hi-Crops in August 1954. *Mike Mack*

Besides a great restoration job, this 1953 Model 50 has other features worth noting, including the rear wheels with the five large openings, which are sometimes referred to as windowpane wheels. Another seldom-seen option are the front wheel weights.

Mike Mack, in charge of developing the Model 40 Hi-Crop, explained how it evolved. "We prototype-tested it in Florida. That was my first big assignment. These final drives came out and had a very, very deep drop housing. That got the back end up in the air, so we had to go to the front end and build much longer spindles. When it got the front elevated, it meant the hitch was way out of whack, way too far from the implement. So I had to redesign the three-point hitch completely.

The Model 50 is the successor to John Deere's best-selling tractor, the Model B. One of the Model 50 features, duplex carburetion, squeezed three extra horsepower from the basic Model B engine.

"Then the problem was what to do about the longitudinal stability. Here's this thing up in the air and it's obvious it doesn't have stability either way. So what we did was split the whole chassis and put a cast-iron spacer in between the transmission case and center frame, which was also cast-iron. I think we put around a 7- or 8-inch spacer between the two housings, which stretched it out and gave it more longitudinal stability. The lateral stability was controlled by the tread width. We just controlled the tread adjustment, so you couldn't get it too narrow. I would call it a two-row tractor.

"One of the requirements of a good Hi-Crop tractor was that any kind of an oil leak was intolerable, because there are areas in Florida where they would be going over the gladiolas, and other flowers, and anything which was even suggestive of an oil leak was a serious problem. So we had to be especially careful about making sure that there were no oil leaks.

"For working big-bedded crops, you have to get the tractor belly way up in the air because those beds are pretty tall. I'd never designed a steering system in my life, so I had to dig out the textbooks and find out how you designed the tie-rod geometry and the pitman geometry, all of which had to be unique to a Hi-Crop version. Otherwise, the Hi-Crop was a Model M."

The Hi-Crop 40 tipped the scales at 3,400 pounds in regular dress. It was the highest-priced wheeled Model 40, retailing at $1,700.

Model 40V Special: 1954–1955

"V" is for vegetable, according to some accounts; this tractor is also known as the sweet potato or peanut tractor. The Special represents a near–Hi-Crop vehicle. It featured a narrower stance and 26 inches of clearance, compared to 32 inches for the true Hi-Crop.

It was also lower—61-5/8 versus 67-1/8 inches and shorter than the Model 40H, 124 inches versus 132 inches. The rear-wheel tread was adjustable from 46 to 80 inches, and the front wheels were adjustable from 46 to 66 inches.

This 3,050-pound vehicle came with a 1955 list price of $1,690.

A beautifully restored Model 50, a John Deere flag, and the leaping deer make a fine image. All that's needed is Mom's apple pie, and you'd have the perfect slice of rural Americana. If you look closely you can see the edge of the Roll-O-Matic decal between the front tires—a $45 option on Model 50 tractors.

The business end of this Model 50 lacks the three-point hitch, indicating that it might have been used mostly for drawbar work. Its 27 drawbar horsepower could drag a two-bottom plow, 8 inches deep, through almost any soil.

Model 40C Crawler: 1953–1955

The Model 40 Crawler was a direct descendant of the Lindeman design of the BO Crawler and MC Crawlers. However, it is unclear just how much direct influence the Lindemans had on the 40C Crawler.

Deere & Company purchased the Lindeman Power Equipment Company of Yakima, Washington, in 1945. After the purchase, the Yakima facility continued to manufacture the tracks, which were shipped to Dubuque rather than having the tractor chassis shipped to Yakima. The John Deere Yakima Works was finally closed in 1953.

If you recall, Mike Mack, retired director of Waterloo's Product Engineering Center, commented on the crawler development at Dubuque and suggested that most, if not all, MC and 40C designs originated with Dubuque engineering. And, in the case of the 40C, the tracks were also manufactured at Dubuque.

Equipped with the same engine changes as the other Model 40s, the 40C also benefited from an approximate 15 percent horsepower increase over its predecessor, the MC. Another important upgrade of the Crawler occurred in July 1953, when the original three-roller track was discontinued in favor of either a four- or five-roller design. The regular shoe widths were 10, 12, or 14 inches.

The hoodline height was 50-1/2 inches and the length of the crawler was 102 inches. The three-roller crawler weighed approximately 4,000 pounds, the four-roller approximately 4,125 pounds, and the five-roller approximately 4,560 pounds. The suggested retail price was about $2,241, $2,365, and $2,568, respectively.

The shift from low-grade fuels to gasoline was well under way when the 40 Series debuted, but there was still enough demand for distillates, tractor fuel, and kerosene that an all-fuel engine was offered in all variants of the Model 40. A total of about 1,650 tractors left the Dubuque facility with all-fuel engines. The rarest all-fuel is the Model 40V Special, with only three tractors manufactured; the most popular was the Model 40S Standard, with a production of 653 vehicles.

> **Nebraska Test 505: 40C Crawler**
>
> **Date: 1953   Fuel: Gasoline   HP: 19 Drawbar, 24 Belt**

Model 50: 1952–1956

This replacement for the Model B introduced duplex carburetion and a live PTO. Buyers could have either a gasoline, all-fuel, or LP gas engine on their new Model 50s.

The Model 50 was powered by a reincarnated Model B engine that utilized the 4-11/16x5-1/2-inch bore and stroke of the Model B and spun at the same 1,250 rpm. Nebraska test number 486 gave it 27 drawbar and 30 belt horsepower burning gasoline, 3 more horses at both the drawbar and the belt.

Where did the extra horses come from? Duplex carburetion and Cyclonic Fuel Intake were responsible. Duplex carburetion really wasn't a carburetor for each cylinder, but rather a single two-barrel carburetor, with each barrel supplying identical amounts of the fuel mixture to each cylinder. The Duplex carb wasn't used on the first all-fuel Model 50s but came online in October 1953. Cyclonic Fuel Intake was the name applied to the cast arch, or eyebrow, positioned over the intake valve on each cylinder. This feature improved the air and fuel mix, resulting in more complete combustion within the cylinder, hence more power. This was also used in the Model 40 engine.

Besides the option of gasoline or all-fuel, the Model 50 could be purchased equipped for LP gas. Five LP gas Model 50s were produced in December 1954, but Model 50s generally became available in 1955. Factory-installed power steering became an option in 1954. The Model 50's predecessor, the Model B, had a 4/1 transmission, but the Model 50 sported a 6/1 with forward speeds ranging from 1-1/2 to 10 miles per hour.

While the Model 40 and Model 60 offered specialty versions such as the Standard, Orchard, and Hi-Crop models in addition to the general-purpose row-crop models, the Model 50

McCORMICK FARMALL SUPER C
1951-1954

Add 10-ci to the engine, plus one Fast Hitch, and "presto," the Farmall C is transformed into the Super C. How super was it? The increased displacement added about 10 percent to the engine's horsepower, and the Fast Hitch no doubt saved more than 10 percent of a farmer's vocabulary when it came time to hook up and head for the field.

After 14 years, International Harvester (IH) finally responded to the Ford-Ferguson three-point hitch in the form of a two-point system that probably was as good as, or better than, the established three-point design. However, the three-point was exactly that: established. IH discontinued the two-point and adopted the industry-accepted three-point system, but only after the Super C's production ended. The Fast Hitch system would only accommodate two-point Fast Hitch implements, which helped IH equipment sales but required customers to invest in a new line of equipment if they purchased a Super C with Fast Hitch. Nevertheless, the Super C sold in very respectable numbers, a total of about 112,000 copies.

The 10 percent increase in horsepower came from an IH-built vertical four-cylinder engine available in either a gasoline or kerosene version. The bore and stroke on the kerosene engine was 3x4 inches, which netted 112.96-ci. The gasoline version used a 3-1/8x4-inch bore and stroke, which upped the cubic inches to 122.56, or 113 and 123, respectively. Both engines were rated at 1,650 rpm. The Super C used a 4/1 transmission capable of forward travel of 2-1/2 to 10-1/2 miles per hour.

Standard equipment included a battery ignition, starter and lights, tricycle front axle, deluxe foam rubber seat, disc brakes, hydraulic system, and gasoline engine. Some options offered were a kerosene (distillate) engine, magneto ignition, fenders, adjustable wide front axle, single front wheel, extrawide rear axle, and Fast Hitch.

The cost of a Super C in 1954 was $1,475. If you planned to haul it to the farmstead, you would need a trailer that could handle all of the Super C's 3,209 pounds.

> **Nebraska Test 458: McCormick Farmall Super C**
> **Date: 1951 Fuel: Gasoline HP: 20 Drawbar, 23 Belt**

was strictly a general-purpose row-crop tractor. Interchangeable front-axle options included single wheel, dual front-wheel tricycle, dual Roll-O-Matic tricycle, wide-fixed 38-inch, and wide-adjustable. Equipped with the wide-adjustable front axle, the tread width could be set from 48 to 80 inches. The rear-tread width, depending on axle choices, varied from 56 to 104 inches.

The Model 50 weighed in between 4,435 and 4,855 pounds and carried a 1954 list price of $2,100. All serial numbers for the Model 50 Series began with 5000001, and production numbers read as follows: 731 LP gas tractors, 2,095 all-fuel vehicles, and 29,748 gasoline copies. The total number of Model 50s produced adds up to 32,574.

The Model 40 and Model 50 tractors offered more power, more operator comfort, and more muscle-saving features than any previous John Deere tractors. Even though Deere was still running in second place behind International Harvester, these tractors were as advanced as any in the field.

> **Nebraska Test 486: Model 50**
> **Date: 1952 Fuel: Gasoline HP: 27 Drawbar, 30 Belt**
> **Nebraska Test 507: Model 50**
> **Date: 1953 Fuel: Tractor Fuel HP: 22 Drawbar, 24 Belt**
> **Nebraska Test 540: Model 50**
> **Date: 1955 Fuel: LP Gas HP: 28 Drawbar, 31 Belt**

Chapter 5

HORSES AND MULES ARE PUT OUT TO PASTURE

Models 320 and 330

The 1950s were years of rapid change for the American farmer, as the postwar boom kicked agriculture into high gear. Agricultural equipment manufacturers were challenged to provide equipment that could keep pace with demand. Customers wanted tractors with more horsepower, and better transmissions, plus advanced operator comfort and convenience. In addition to the improved function of the tractor, form was becoming increasingly important, with tractor manufacturers who chose to ignore looks doing so at their own peril. So rapid was the change that, almost simultaneous with the introduction of its Numbered Series Tractors, Deere & Company made a decision that all but rendered the series obsolete before the farmer had a chance to break his tractor in properly.

Previous pages

From this vantage point, this Model 320 Standard appears to have more than 21 inches of clearance under the front axle. The adjustable axle could be set from 40 to 55 inches.

After much head scratching, arguing, and soul searching, in 1953 Deere management mandated that four- and six-cylinder powerplants would soon replace the beloved two-cylinder engine. The era of the "Johnny Popper" was coming to a close, but it would take until 1960 before the company could design, tool up, and begin producing these New Generation tractors. Finding a way to make the transition without destroying the company presented Deere's management with one of its biggest challenges.

Deere & Company President Charles Deere Wiman died on May 12, 1955. Less than two weeks later, William Hewitt, Wiman's son-in-law, was elected as the sixth president of

Deere & Company. Hewitt had been at his new post only a few days when he announced that Deere was "aiming to be first in all our business activities." Deere, which at this time was still second to International Harvester, would, if Hewitt had his way, soon be number one in the agricultural machinery industry.

The timeline for the 20 Series tractors began with the Dubuque-built 420 Series, introduced in November 1955. In August 1956, the Waterloo-built 520, 620, 720, and 820 Models were introduced along with the Dubuque-built Model 320 Series.

MODEL 320: 1956–1958

Built in Dubuque, Iowa, the Model 320 Standard and Model 320 Utility tractors offered many mechanical upgrades and improvements, while still filling the low purchase cost and low production cost slot in Deere's agricultural and industrial line.

The Model 320's family lineage goes back to the Model M and the Model 40. The Model 40 became the Model 420, while

This straight-steer 1956 Model 320 Utility is fitted with an orchard muffler. It presents a clean, low profile that's ideal for working inside farm buildings with low overhead clearance.

were fewer potential tractor customers. The industry would never again see the heady years with production numbers in the hundreds of thousand for a single model.

The Model 320 was never tested at Nebraska, so we don't officially know its true horsepower. Deere rated it at 21.5 belt horsepower; another source puts it closer to 22; and a third source says horsepower results were based on the Model 40 Nebraska test results, which would ascribe 24 belt horsepower to the Model 320.

According to Brent Sampson of the Nebraska Tractor Test Laboratory, it appears that the best "unofficial official" numbers are those of test number 387. Sampson said that since the 320 used the same engine (the same manufacturer, same displacement, and same rpm) as the Model M, the 1947 Model M test results apply to the Model 320 and 330. Nebraska Test Laboratory's document, *List of Tractors Tested or Summarized at the Nebraska Tractor Test Laboratory*, lists the John Deere 320 and 330 as test number 387.

Nebraska Test 387: Model 320 Industrial

Date: 1957   Fuel: Gasoline   HP: 18 Drawbar, 20 Belt

The vertical two-cylinder Deere-built engine had a 4x4-inch bore and stroke, yielding 101-ci of displacement and rated at 1,650 rpm. The 4/1 transmission gave forward speeds of 1-5/8 to 12 miles per hour.

The cooling system was a simple thermosiphon, although Deere advertising material spelled it Thermo-Siphon, which suggests that marketing intended to present it as a Deere feature, as the company did with Powr-Trol and Touch-O-Matic. The 320 Series fielded only four variants—the Standard, the Utility, the Industrial, and the Special, or "V," model. They were available with two different fuel options—gasoline or all-fuel.

One other distinct design feature that divides this series from others was the straight-steer and slant-steer versions, which refer to the steering wheel's position of either straight up-and-down vertical or slanted with the top forward. Although not deemed absolutely necessary on the small Dubuque tractors, power steering was offered as an option beginning with 1958 models.

Model 320 Standard: 1956–1958

The Standard was the sales leader among the Model 320 tractors by a two-to-one margin, with 2,167 vehicles produced. The breakdown of variants included 1,836 straight-steer gas; 12 straight-steer all-fuel; 317 slant-steer gas; and 2 slant-steer all-fuel.

The standard equipment included a three-point hitch system, Load-and-Depth Control, electric starter, battery,

This 1957 Model 320 Standard with serial number 320563 was shipped to Russell, Kansas, and has never been more than 100 miles away from Russell in all its 44 years.

the Model 320 and 330 retained many of the Model M components and borrowed others from the Model 40. Styling did not radically depart from the Model M or Model 40, although the yellow band added to the hood and radiator cowling made the 320s appear as a completely new line of tractors. It was vital that these new tractors convince customers, and the competition, that Deere was committed to the continuance of the two-cylinder tradition.

With only 3,084 copies of the Model 320 produced, the first impression might be that sales were disappointing. It is important to remember, however, that during this time the number of American farms was declining, while the amount of work a single tractor could perform was increasing. Also, the switch from horses and mules to tractors as farm power had been achieved almost universally by this time, so there

HORSE AND MULE POPULATION

How many horses and mules were on American farms when tractors began to replace them as a means of doing field work and other chores? Of course, nobody knows the exact figures, but the best source is the U.S. Bureau of the Census. These Census results were reported in *The Statistical History of the United States from Colonial Times to the Present.*

The following figures include all horses and mules that were reported in the census for these years, including colts:

	Horses	Mules
1900	16,965,000	3,039,000
1910	19,220,000	4,101,000
1918	21,238,000	5,485,000
1920	19,767,000	5,432,000
1930	13,384,000	5,354,000
1940	10,087,000	3,845,000
1950	5,402,000	2,202,000
1957	3,574,000*	

*Beginning in 1951, horses and mules combined.

The same reference work provided the following figures for work stock, over 27 months old, on farms between 1920 to 1957:

1920	22,386,000
1930	17,612,000
1940	13,029,000
1950	7,415,000
1957	3,380,000

generator, adjustable front axle, adjustable cushioned seat, adjustable back rest, transmission-driven PTO, fenders, water temperature gauge, oil pressure gauge, fuel filter, oil filter, and air cleaner. The front axle was adjustable from 40 to 55 inches, while the rear tread could be adjusted from 38-3/4 to 54-1/4 inches. With the final drive assemblies positioned downward and its taller front axle spindles, the Standard model had 21 inches of crop clearance. As with its predecessor, the Model M, the Model 320 was equipped with an automotive-type foot clutch and disk-type foot-operated brakes.

Some of the options available to customize a Model 320 to the customer's specific needs included an all-fuel engine, high-altitude engine, lighting package, orchard muffler, exhaust silencer, underneath/rear exhaust system, dual Touch-O-Matic hydraulic system, remote hydraulic control, dry-charge battery, yellow seat upholstery, rear-mounted belt pulley, foot throttle, hydraulic tractor jack, precleaner, PTO stub shaft, radiator shutter, remote hydraulic cylinder, safety warning lamp and

Continues on page 102

A 1956 Model 320 Utility, such as the one pictured here, made an excellent agricultural haying tractor or a great mowing vehicle for maintaining highway right-of-ways. At a 1958 price of $1,885, it was an economical way to do both.

The final drives on this 1957 Model 320 Utility are rotated 90 degrees, as on the Model M Utility. It's the secret to the tractor's low, stable stance. The three-point hitch was standard equipment, but if the customer preferred, he could order his tractor without one.

OLIVER SUPER 55
1954-1958

The Super 55 was Oliver's first true small utility tractor, and Oliver engineers used the Ford 8N as its benchmark for its design. It was also Oliver's first small utility tractor with a three-point hitch and draft control.

However, before the Super 55 was introduced, Ford launched its NAA Jubilee model, in 1953, which featured a larger engine and improved hydraulic system. Oliver responded by using the same engine as the larger Oliver Super 66 engine, super-quiet helical transmission gears, an independent PTO, and integral hydraulic system for three-point- mounted equipment.

Oliver was an early leader in diesel-powered tractors, and the Super 55 was one of the industry's first small utility tractors powered by diesel. The engine was a four-cylinder Oliver/Waukesha-built powerplant, with the diesel version offering a 15-3/4:1 compression ratio. The gasoline version provided a 7:1 compression ratio, which was extremely high but yielded improved performance and economy. The engine's 3-1/2x3-3/4-inch bore and stroke displaced 144-ci. The rated rpm for drawbar work was 1,750, while for belt work the rpm could be increased to 2,000 rpm. The 6/2 transmission gave working and travel speeds of 1-11/16 to 13-3/16 miles per hour and 1-7/8 or 3-7/8 miles per hour in reverse. Like the Ford 8N that Oliver used as a pattern, the Super 55's hydraulic system was designed into the transmission. Standard features included an electric starter, electric lights, PTO, and belt pulley.

Power steering was available as an option on all Super 55 vehicles. The agricultural model came with an adjustable wide front axle, allowing tread width of 48 to 76 inches. An industrial version of the Super 55 was available. It offered virtually identical features as the agricultural model, except the front axle was a fixed standard tread, and the industrial came equipped with a foot accelerator. The diesel model weighed in at 2,933 pounds, which was about 100 pounds heavier than the gasoline model.

The gasoline version carried a price tag of about $2,075, while the diesel version was $2,560.

Nebraska Test 524: Oliver Super 55
Date: 1954   Fuel: Gasoline   HP: 29 Drawbar, 34 Belt
Nebraska Test 526: Oliver Super 55
Date: 1954   Fuel: Diesel   HP: 27 Drawbar, 33 Belt

ALLIS-CHALMERS D-14
1957-1960

Allis-Chalmers' (AC) tractor line received a major overhaul in 1957. The Model B had been in the line for two decades, and the Model CA was nine years into production. The new tractors for the year were part of the D line, with the D-14 being the small tractor of the bunch when it was introduced in 1957.

Perhaps it isn't an apple-to-apple comparison with other small utility tractors (it weighed almost 900 pounds more than the John Deere Model 320 and the engine had about 50 percent more cubic inches), but it did exemplify the trend in small tractors. Manufacturers were offering more bang for your buck—more power plus more operator comfort and convenience. And transmissions were undergoing some major changes, too, such as a wider gear selection and shift-on-the-go ability.

Almost all the major components of the D-14 were of a new design for AC tractors. The styling got a facelift with the D Series, the AC-designed-and-built engine was new, and the 8/2 transmission with Power-Director was also a first.

Offered in gasoline and LP gas versions, the new four-cylinder engine featured a 3-1/2x3 7/8-inch bore and stroke, which garnered 149-ci of displacement. The rated rpm was 1,650 for both gasoline and LP gas. However, the compression ratio for gasoline was 7.5:1, while the LP gas version was 8.5:1.

Foremost among the new features of the D-14 was the Power-Director hand clutch, which activated a high or low range on the constant-mesh four-speed transmission. This effectively provided eight forward and two reverse speeds, with high-low on-the-go shifting. The natural position of the hand clutch stopped ground travel but allowed the PTO to continue running.

Several versions of the D-14 were offered, including a dual-front-wheel tricycle, adjustable wide front axle, single-front-wheel, high clearance, and orchard. The tread-width adjustment ranged from 54 to 80 inches. Other goodies were the Power-Shift rear-wheel adjustment, Roll-Shift front-axle adjustment, optional integral power steering, and improved seat location and suspension.

The total production of the D-14 tallied 22,292 units, with the orchard version carrying a list price of $3,770.

Allis-Chalmers refused (or neglected) to quickly capitulate to the universal acceptance of the three-point hitch and instead offered its own Snap Coupling system of implement attachment, which no doubt restricted sales.

> Nebraska Test 623: Allis-Chalmers D-14
> Date: 1957   Fuel: Gasoline   HP: 30 Drawbar, 34 Belt Power-Director PRPS (2) Transmission

Continued from page 98

mast, inner-front frame weight, outer frame weight, and rear wheel weights.

The shipping weight on the 320 Standard was 2,650 pounds, and the price tag weighed in at $1,805 for the basic no-option tractor. The serial numbers for the straight-steer Standard 320 begin with 320001 and end with 322566. Slant-steer numbers start at 325001 and run through 325517.

Model 320 Utility: 1956–1958

For the Model 320 Utility, there were 917 sold, broken down as follows: 716 straight-steer gasoline; two straight-steer all-fuel; and 199 slant-steer gasoline. Not one slant-steer all-fuel tractor was produced.

This vehicle's low-slung stance offered only 11 inches of axle clearance, but its low profile—only 50 inches at the hoodline—made it an excellent tractor for field, orchard, and vineyard applications.

This rear-wheel weight on a Model 320 listed for about $18 when the tractor was new in 1957.

The 1958 price for the optional orchard muffler, such as the one on this unit, was $9.45. The lighting package set the customer back $28.

You might have found Model 320 tractors that used the thermosiphon cooling system nuzzled up to an old cistern pump such as this when the tractor needed a drink on a hot summer day. And yes, that was the only water source for the house on some farms in the 1950s.

The Utility carried the same specs as the Standard, with a couple of notable exceptions. The Utility tractor could be ordered minus the three-point hitch system, and Dual Touch-O-Matic was not an option, as it was on the Standard model.

The Utility model weighed in at 2,750 pounds, and the listed price for the no-option model was $1,885. The straight-steer Utility serial numbers begin with 320017 and end with 322562. Slant-steer numbers range between 325004 and 325518.

Model 320V Special: 1956–1958

Records indicate that Deere accommodated some customers with a one-off special version of the Model 320, the finished product being an estimated 60 to 70 Standard tractors that were converted to Southern Specials or V vehicles. These special high-clearance models were the result of marrying 10-34 rear tires, fenders, drawbar, hitch, and front axles from the 420 V to the Model 320 Standard. The added crop clearance made it desirable for specialty cultivation for bedded crops.

Model 320 Industrial: 1956–1958

A low center of gravity, a coat of yellow or orange paint, and a mounted mower made the Model 320 Industrial a popular tractor for state and county maintenance of highway right-of-ways. The Industrial's serial numbers fall within the Utility model numbers, therefore the exact number produced isn't known.

Model 330: 1958–1960

The mechanics of the 30 Series tractors were virtually identical to their 20 Series predecessors. Deere heralded the series as the "New John Deere," and the difference was primarily in appearance, comfort, and convenience. Deere & Company personnel who were privy to the New Generation project hoped these new features would allay any concerns that Deere was about to abandon the trusty two-cylinder.

Cosmetically, the basic theme stayed the same as the 20 Series—John Deere green and John Deere yellow, with

FORD 681 DIESEL: 1957-1961

In 1955, Ford abandoned its "one tractor fits all" philosophy and introduced the 100 Series line, featuring the 600, 700, 800, and 900 model tractors. In 1957, the 100 Series was replaced by the 101 Series; the Workmaster and Powermaster 601, 701, 801; and 901 Series tractors. These were also the first Ford tractors to offer the same fuel options as most of the competition: gasoline, diesel, and LP gas.

In 1959, 20 years after launching the famous 9N, Ford, perhaps envisioning future heydays reminiscent of the Fordson, once again stepped up its efforts to be a major player in the tractor business. Management plowed $6.7 million into renovation of its Highland Park, Michigan, plant. This ambitious program led Ford to develop a new transmission, which proved extremely troublesome when it was first introduced on the Model 801 Series and was made available on the 601 tractors. The new Select-O-Speed transmission was hydraulically shifted through four planetary gear sets, providing 10 forward and 2 reverse shift-on-the-go speeds.

The Ford-built Red Tiger engine introduced in the NAA Golden Jubilee made the transition to the Model 681. It was 134-ci with a 3-7/16x3-5/8-inch bore and stroke for the gasoline and LP gas versions. The diesel engine upped the cubic inches to 144 from a 3-9/16x3- 5/8-inch bore and stroke. All versions revved at the same 2,200 rated rpm. The diesel version was equipped with a 12-volt system, while the gasoline and LP gas models used the 6-volt system.

Under standard equipment listed for the Model 681 was a generator, battery, oil bath air cleaner, oil filter, muffler, fenders, oil pressure gauge, fuel gauge, temperature gauge, generator warning light, starter, key ignition, hydraulic system, three-point linkage, and Select-O-Speed transmission with 540 and 1,000 rpm independent PTO.

The shipping weight was approximately 2,812 pounds.

Nebraska Test 706: Ford 681 Diesel

Date: 1959 Fuel: Diesel HP: 25 Drawbar, 31 Belt PSH Transmission

---

Industrial yellow applied as needed. However, industrial designer Henry Dreyfuss and his team supplied some notable styling and comfort changes that marketing could tout. Now they had some sizzle to sell! The hoodline was changed, as was its yellow accent. The model number's typeface was changed and moved to high on the side of the radiator cowl.

The dash also received a new look and arrangement. Its forward slant and slanted steering wheel changed the tractor's side profile dramatically and placed the gauges in an easy-to-read position.

Style sometimes comes at considerable cost and frustration when it's transferred from the drawing board to the production floor. Such was the case involving the nose cowl, where the leaping deer badge was affixed on the 30 Series tractors. Robert P. Guetzlaff, retired fabrication manager for Deere, explained how difficult it was to form the "hog nose," or "hog snout." Each time a cowl was pressed in the die, it came out with a stress fracture on the hog nose. The solution for achieving acceptable cowls, which was the only way to let

Continues on page 108

From front to back, this collection of 30 Series tractors includes a 1959 Utility, a 1959 Standard, and a 1959 Special. The restoration job is textbook original on all three vehicles.

This Model 330 Standard is equipped with lots of goodies, including rear-wheel weights and front-frame weight. Black was the standard color for the seat upholstery, but this unit has the no-cost option of yellow.

INTERNATIONAL HARVESTER FARMALL 130 SERIES: 1956-1958

A strong competitor to the John Deere Model 320, the Farmall 130 Series tractors outsold its green and yellow rivals by almost a three-to-one margin, with total production of the Farmall 130 Series registering 9,197 copies.

By the mid-1950s, hand cranking was mostly a memory, except for operators still using older tractors. For certain, owners didn't have an old tractor in the Farmall 130, and they didn't have to crank. The battery ignition, starter, and lights were standard equipment. Other standard amenities included Touch Control hydraulics, Fast Hitch, muffler, adjustable front axle, and fenders. A bevy of optional equipment was available, including a belt pulley and PTO, wheel weights, deluxe seat, distillate/kerosene engine, magneto ignition, and nonadjustable front axle.

The tread width varied from 44 to 64 inches on the front axle and 40 to 68 inches on the rear axle. The Hi-Clearance version of the Farmall 130 provided 27-1/2 inches of clearance, which was 6 inches more than the regular Farmall 130. The tread width was 48 to 68 inches on the rear axle and 43-3/4 to 67-3/4 inches on the front axle.

International Harvester manufactured its own engine for the Farmall 130 Series, the popular vertical I-head four-cylinder with 123-ci. The bore and stroke was 3-1/8x4 inches and the gasoline powerplant was rated at 1,400 rpm. A 4/1 tranny allowed forward travel of 2-1/3, 3- 3/4, 4-13/16, and 10 miles per hour.

The stock vehicle weighed approximately 2,710 pounds and listed in the neighborhood of $1,950.

> **Nebraska Test 617: Farmall 130 Series**
>
> **Date: 1957   Fuel: Gasoline   HP: 19 Drawbar, 22 Belt**

The slanted dash and steering wheel on this Model 330 Utility tractor represent the final stage in the evolution of the straight-versus-slanted-dash and steering wheel, which began with the 20 Series tractors. Notice there is still a hole for the all-fuel control and the knock-out for the speed-hour meter.

Left

This 1959 Model 330 Utility is 1 of 247 produced during the last two years of the two-cylinder era.

W hether you call this Model 330 the V, Special, or Southern Special, you must also call it rare. Just how rare isn't known. Researchers and collectors haven't finalized the count, but they estimate that from 20 to 75 units were built around the Model 330 Standard tractor.

Continued from page 104

the tractors roll off the assembly line, was to preheat each piece with a hand torch before it went into the press. This labor-intensive solution was used until a heating unit was designed, one that quickly heated the sheet metal before it was formed in the press.

Many of these small design changes were really the Dreyfuss team's experiments, simply perfecting features that would ultimately appear on the New Generation tractors. A case in point was the seat evolution. Dreyfuss engaged human posture specialist Dr. Janet Travell, who gained nationwide recognition for treating John Kennedy's persistent back problems, to design the ultimate in operator-friendly seats.

T his outer front-frame weight tipped the scales at 148 pounds and cost $21.25.

HORSEPOWER

Manufacturers proudly advertise horsepower figures for their tractors and often engage the Nebraska Tractor Test Laboratory to verify how many "official" horses are under the hood. Potential customers like to know a tractor's horsepower rating to judge the amount of work it can be expected to do, or perhaps to establish bragging rights down at the local co-op. For certain, horsepower ratings are sprinkled liberally, like a stock recipe ingredient, throughout magazine articles and books about tractors. But, unless everyone is on the same page, these ratings can cloud the issue. There's more than one kind of horsepower, and knowing which one is given is imperative. The following are explanations of the different horsepower ratings:

Drawbar horsepower—The power, or "pull," at the drawbar of the tractor. Some of the engine's power is used to operate systems such as the hydraulic system and electrical system and will therefore be 10 to 15 percent lower than the gross or net engine rating.

PTO horsepower—How much power is available at the tractor's PTO. PTO tests began at Nebraska in 1959.

Belt horsepower—The power available to run a belt-driven machine. The power from a belt is about 1 to 2 percent less than at the PTO because of belt slippage. Belt horsepower tests were discontinued when the PTO tests began.

Gross horsepower—The power at the flywheel of an engine having only the components necessary for it to run.

Net brake horsepower—The power at the flywheel of an engine fitted with all its components and able to run by itself.

SAE horsepower—The formula used by the Society of Automotive Engineers, which determines the approximate brake horsepower of an engine. The SAE rating is 85 percent of the adjusted belt/PTO horsepower and 75 percent of the adjusted drawbar horsepower. Nebraska discontinued this rating in 1960.

Corrected brake horsepower—A formula is used to correct the observed brake horsepower to account for altitude, temperature, humidity, and barometric pressure. This corrects the tests to 60 degrees Fahrenheit and 30 inches of mercury.

Observed brake horsepower—The power output of an engine operating under the actual air, temperature, humidity, and barometric conditions when the test is conducted.

A company's horsepower ratings pre-Nebraska tests were understandably given the benefit of the doubt on the high end, and were often rerated when the tractor was officially tested at Nebraska. The ratings in this book are from the Nebraska Tractor Test Laboratory unless stated otherwise. They are maximum observed and truncated, or rounded down, to the nearest whole number.

A close-up of the "hog nose" that proved a real challenge for personnel in Deere's Manufacturing Engineering Department.

The result of her work with Deere & Company was a tractor seat that provided vastly improved comfort and safety. The safety factor surfaced when tests revealed that the maximum safe up-and-down movement of the seat was 4 inches. Movement greater than 4 inches jeopardized the ability of the operator to remain on the seat and to control the tractor. Owners who purchased a 30 Series tractor were literally sitting on advanced features of the New Generation tractors.

One noted mechanical difference was that while the Model 320 Series could be purchased with an all-fuel engine, the Model 330 tractors were available only as gas burners.

For drivetrain specs, standard equipment, and options, refer to the corresponding Model 320 tractors, discussed previously in this chapter.

Model 330 Standard: 1958–1960

All variants of the Model 330 were serial numbered between 330001 and 331091. The final tally for 330 Standard production totaled 844 copies, and the base price for a no-option Model 330 Standard was $1,985.

Model 330 Utility: 1958–1960

This was a relatively low-production vehicle, with only 247 copies made. At approximately 2,750 pounds, the 330U was about 100 pounds heavier than the Standard model, but it sold for $300 less—$1,685—for the basic tractor.

Model 330 Industrial: 1958–1960

The industrial models of the 330 were basically the same tractor as the 430 Industrial, with the exception of the engine. The Model 330 Industrial was fitted with a smaller engine, and it filled an important slot in Deere's Industrial Division. This tractor emphasized economy of purchase and operation, while the 430 Industrial was more about horsepower.

Model 330V Special: 1958–1960

Although not an official Deere & Company product, a few of these exist. As far as where these tractors came from if they're not an official Deere product, the best theory is that they are 330 Standard tractors converted with parts from a Model 40V or a Model 420V. The weight would probably be about the same as the 320V or 420V with the price a bit higher.

It is interesting to note that by 1958, when the last two-cylinder tractors were introduced, the use of animals as a major source of power on the farm was coming to a close. But both the two-cylinder John Deere tractor and the workhorse would assume new roles in the years ahead.

Model 330 Specials, such as this 1959 example, were sometimes call Semi Hi-Crops because of the extra 5-1/2 inches of clearance under the axles, compared to the Standard model's clearance.

Chapter 6

THE END OF AN ERA

Models 420, 430, and 435

A s the 1950s drew to a close, the number of work animals on the nation's farms dropped to about 3.3 million, down from a high of 26.7 million in 1918. Meanwhile, the number of tractors rose from approximately 2,000 in 1910 to 3,609,281 by 1950.

It was a decisive victory for mechanical horsepower over four-footed horsepower. Were there no further challenges for tractor manufacturers? The demise of the horse and mule teams was a welcome byproduct of an industry obsessed with producing bigger and better farm tractors.

Only 212 copies of the Model 430 Hi-Crop were produced by the Dubuque factory. All were gasoline burners. Almost twice as many were produced in 1959 as in 1960—141 versus 71.

These tractors not only enabled fewer agricultural personnel to produce more product, but also allowed the tractor manufacturers to survive in an increasingly highly capitalized and competitive industry. The stakes were spiraling higher and higher. The key to survival was a superior product.

For Deere & Company, the stakes were even higher. It was imperative that the two-cylinder tractor line be competitive and profitable, even though the New Generation multicylinder tractors were secretly being engineered as replacements for the venerated two-lungers. Any hard evidence that the two-cylinder 20 and 30 Series tractors were soon to be obsolete would have killed sales and possibly killed the company.

MODEL 420 SERIES: 1956–1958

Any way you want it. This aptly describes the 420 tractor, which was available in a bevy of models, including the Tricycle, which featured a single-wheel and wide-axle front end; the Standard; the Hi-Crop, which had a 32-inch clearance; the Special, with its 27-inch clearance and multiple wheel spacing; plus the Utility, Orchard, and Crawler.

The Dubuque-built Model 420 Series debuted in November 1955, the first of the 20 Series, and was followed eight months later by the remainder of the 20 Series line. Production of the 420 Series can be divided into three distinct groups or phases.

Phase One

Phase one 420 tractors were essentially dead ringers of the Model 20's predecessor, the Model 40. All green tinwork, yellow wheels, and a chrome-plated "John Deere" medallion on the upper grille serve as identification points for the phase one 420 Series.

This phase three slant-steer Model 420 Utility could be either a 1957 or 1958 model. If you go by the build date, it would be a 1957 tractor, but if you go by the calendar year, it would be a 1958 model.

MINNEAPOLIS-MOLINE 335
1956-1961

In the late 1940s, Minneapolis-Moline (MM) experienced record sales and growth, in part due to the seemingly insatiable postwar demand for tractors–and also because of the company's well-built, dependable products. Management's optimism concerning future growth led to a merger with the B. F. Avery Company in March 1951. MM was the surviving company. Avery's Louisville facility added needed production capacity plus a ready-made line of small tractors. However, the Korean War spoiled MM's plans. The federal government's defense production requirements and materials controls forced MM to sell the Louisville plant in 1955, after suffering losses in the millions of dollars.

The production of the MM/Avery small tractor was discontinued in 1955—from that day on MM never again had a small-tractor line. The Model 335, which was introduced in 1956, became the baby of the Prairie Gold fleet.

Initially, only a gasoline engine was offered for the Model 335, but within a short time an LP gas version was also produced. The same MM-built vertical four-cylinder engine was used in both versions. The rated rpm was 1,600 and its 3-5/8x4-inch bore and stroke provided 165-ci, which made it a small tractor with big power.

Specification sheets list two different groups of features customers could choose from to customize a Model 335 for their specific agricultural or industrial needs. The extra equipment included a PTO, auxiliary PTO located under the transmission for side- and front-mounted equipment, belt pulley, rear wheel weights, front wheel weights, and a built-in hydraulic unit with cylinder.

Additional options were Power Adjustable rear wheels, remote jack, power steering, and three-point hitch. But perhaps the most heralded option was the 10/2 Ampli-Torc transmission, which provided 10 forward and two reverse gears. In reality, it was just MM's trusty 5/1 transmission with a low range that could be engaged on-the-go to provide extra torque for tough loads.

The Universal, or tricycle, Model 335 was brought online in 1957 and stayed through 1959. The engine and tranny specs were the same as the Utility model.

Also in 1957, the Model 335 Industrial Wheel Tractor began production, which lasted through 1960. It shared many features and specs with the agricultural model, but there were some notable exceptions. Initially the Industrial was available with the 5/1 transmission only, but soon a shuttle transmission was offered, which provided five forward and five reverse speeds. It is believed that the shuttle tranny became standard equipment on late-production units.

On the Utility Model 335, the tread-width adjustment ranged from 48 to 76 inches. Forward speeds fell between 2-3/4 and 15 miles per hour.

Although it remained in production for five years, only 2,539 of the Model 335 were produced. The Model 335 weighed approximately 3,070 pounds and listed at about $2,500.

Nebraska Test 624: MM 335

Date: 1957 Fuel: Gasoline   HP: 29 Drawbar, 33 Belt Power-Director PRPS (2) Transmission

A 1956 Model 420 Row-Crop Utility (W). This tractor would be correct with either the all-green or green and yellow paint scheme, because Deere made the change in midyear and the serial number 83451 is just about in the middle. The speed-hour meter has only 1,554 original hours.

Phase Two

Phase two saw the production of seven different versions of the Model 420: the Standard, Utility, Tricycle, Row-Crop Utility, Hi-Crop, Special, and Crawler. Phase two tractors had a yellow vertical and horizontal stripe on the hood, and the chrome "John Deere" was replaced with the leaping Deere badge, which gave these vehicles a spiffy new look. In addition, an Industrial-Version Special Utility (I) was added to the original seven models.

Phase Three

With the exception of the Hi-Crop and LP Gas tractors, phase three tractors featured a slant steering wheel

This Model 420's dash still has the same two empty holes as the Model 40 shown earlier, because an all-fuel engine was still being offered. The thermosiphon cooling system was replaced with a water pump and pressurized system on the 420s, but the place for a radiator shutter control remained on the dash.

It cost $20 to add this optional weight to the front frame of a Model 420. The extra weight helped keep the front end on the ground when a piece of heavy equipment was mounted on the three-point hitch.

and automotive dash. Phase three also marked the first time production power steering was offered as an option on wheeled models. Also standard on all versions was the Deere-built vertical two-cylinder I-head engine with a 4-1/4x4-inch bore and stroke that yielded 113ci. This was an 1/4-inch increase in the bore, which added 12-ci of displacement over the Model 40 powerplant. The rpm remained at 1,850.

Additional under-the-hood changes and improvements included increased compression ratios, combustion chamber changes for better mixture and combustion, plus a new carburetor. The thermosiphon cooling system wasn't adequate for the 420 Series' higher horsepower, so it used a water pump and a pressurized system.

An advertising brochure touted these features of the 420 tractors: "Handy 'live' Touch-O-Matic hydraulic system and Load-and-Depth Control are built-in features of all '420' wheel-type tractors, as is the convenient, time-saving standard three-point hitch."

The Dubuque facility, perhaps more than other Deere plants, produced custom orders for buyers. Thus, what was standard and what was optional occasionally blurred. That said, most of the following options were available for all models: all-fuel engine, LP gas engine, live PTO, five-speed transmission, fenders, belt pulley, power steering, directional reverser, orchard muffler, silencer muffler, remote hydraulic control, remote cylinder, front- and rear-wheel weights, power-adjust rear wheels, and hour meter. A no-cost option for all Crawlers and Utilities was an industrial-yellow paint job. In fact, the same yellow paint was available as a special order for any of the 420 tractors.

Deere & Company made sure that regardless of which Model 420 a customer purchased, there was a matching Deere implement designed and manufactured to handle *any* farming operation, regardless of size. The list included at least three dozen implements and attachments, from plows to planters, and peanut pullers to cotton pickers, to corn shellers and cultivators.

The 420 models were good sellers, with a total of 46,450 vehicles rolling off the Dubuque assembly lines.

MODEL 420 CRAWLER: 1956–1958

The demand for track-laying vehicles to work boggy fields, orchards, groves, and industrial sites resulted in more sales for the 420 Crawler than any of its wheeled siblings. The total production for all phases reached 17,882 vehicles, which included both the four-roller and five-roller versions of the Crawler.

Fitted with a 4/1 transmission, it offered forward travel of 7/8, 2-1/4, 3, and 5-1/4 miles per hour with a reverse

INTERNATIONAL HARVESTER INTERNATIONAL B-275 DIESEL 1959-1964

Another trend that was emerging among agricultural equipment companies was the manufacturing of tractors in facilities outside of the United States. This was an effort to reduce the cost of production, especially on the small tractors, which didn't have the large profit margin of the higher-priced models.

The B-275 Diesel was built in the United Kingdom by the International Harvester (IH) Company of Great Britain in London. This plant was primarily intended to supply a worldwide market exclusive of North America. However, by 1957 the B-275 was being imported to Canada, and by 1959 this tractor had secured a beachhead at Jacksonville, Florida, from where it was marketed primarily throughout the southeastern United States. This British model was powered by an IH-built vertical four-cylinder engine with a 3-3/8x4-inch bore and stroke. Displacement totaled 144-ci, and the rated rpm was 1,875. A 4/1 transmission with a Hi-Lo range provided an 8/2 transmission with forward speeds from 1.6 to 14 miles per hour. The tread width could be adjusted from 48 to 76 inches.

Standard equipment included a live PTO, disc brakes, 12-volt electrical system, live hydraulics, and three-point hitch. A High-Crop version was produced beginning in 1958. It is unknown if any of these vehicles reached the United States.

The B-275 weighed approximately 3,600 pounds and carried a price in the neighborhood of $2,800.

Nebraska Test 733: International Harvester International B-275

Date: 1960 Fuel: Diesel   HP: 30 Drawbar, 32 Belt

---

speed of 1-3/4 miles per hour. The track-shoe width could be 10, 12, or 14 inches, with regular tread width from 38 to 44 inches.

With phase two production, a three-point hitch was made available as an option. This same hitch could be retrofitted to earlier-phase Model 420 Crawlers and even the Model 40 Crawler.

The four-roller version weighed in at 4,150 pounds, while the five-roller vehicle tipped the scales at 4,700 pounds. The price for a basic Crawler was right around the $2,300 mark.

Phase one Crawler serial numbers range from 80002 to 94815; phase two from 100008 to 119761; and phase three from 125007 to 136795. There were 234 all-fuel and only 4 LP gas Crawlers produced.

Nebraska Test 601: Model 420 Crawler

Date: 1956 Fuel: Gasoline   HP: 23 Drawbar, 28 Belt

Model 420 Row-Crop Utility: 1956–1958

The Model 420 Row-Crop Utility racked up higher production numbers than any other wheeled Model 420, with a total of 11,197 manufactured.

The standard transmission was a 4/1, with a 5/1 offered as an option. The 4/1 provided forward travel of 1.62, 3.12, 4.25, and 12 miles per hour. The 5/1 added a 6.25-miles-per-hour gear, which provided a higher speed for light field work.

A wide row-crop utility, with the emphasis on "wide," describes the stance of the 420 Row-Crop Utility. Fitted with the regular front axle, the tread width was adjustable from 48 to 80 inches. Slap on the optional front axle, and the range varied from 56 to 88 inches.

The regular rear-tread width could be adjusted from 48 to 98 inches or, if the owner opted for the power-adjusted rear wheels, ranged from 56 to 88 inches. It stood taller than the Utility model and offered 21 inches of crop clearance.

With the ability to cultivate up to four rows, perform any job on small-acreage farms, plus do its fair share on big operations, it's no surprise it was a popular model. The vehicle weighed about 2,850 pounds and rang up $2,170 on the cash register.

The serial numbers for phase one 420 Row-Crop Utility tractors are 80179 to 94818; for phase two, 100001 to 119763; and for phase three, 125002 to 136868. There were 399 all-fuel copies of the 420W and 100 LP gas vehicles produced.

Nebraska Test 599: 420 Row-Crop Utility

Date: 1956 Fuel: Gasoline   HP: 26 Drawbar, 28 Belt

Model 420 Tricycle: 1956–1958

With a total of 7,580 manufactured, the Tricycle posted the second-highest production numbers among the Model 420 wheel tractors. Its popularity and versatility were due in part to four interchangeable front ends, which included the dual front-wheel tricycle, the single front wheel, and two wide-adjustable front axles. The square-tube-design front axle

Depending on your perspective, this image of a Model 420 and Model 320 highlights either their similarities or their differences.

J. I. CASE 200 SERIES 1958-1960

Case's new 200 Series tractors were introduced in 1958 to fill the company's small-tractor niche. The Model 210 was a utility tractor, while the Model 211 was a general-purpose vehicle with a tricycle front axle.

Power was provided by Case's vertical L-head four-cylinder engine with 3-1/8x4-1/8-inch bore and stroke, giving 126.5-ci. Compared to earlier Case engines operating at relatively low rpm's, this was a screamer, rated at 1,900 rpm. Gasoline was the only fuel option on the 200 Series.

Manufactured at Case's Rock Island Plant in 1958 and 1959, only 2,022 copies were produced. In keeping with the demand for more transmission speeds and features, several different transmission options were offered in the 200 Series. Initially it carried a 4/1 tranny with the Triple-Range as an option. This option was followed by an 8/1 with synchronized mechanical shuttle, which provided eight forward and eight reverse speeds. Depending on the buyer's preference, the hitch could be Case's Eagle Hitch or a three-point system.

The tractor weight was approximately 3,164 pounds, and customers were required to lay down about $2,490 to add one of these tractors to their farming operation.

> **Nebraska Test 688: J. I. Case 200 Series**
> **Date: 1959 Fuel: Gasoline   HP: 26 Drawbar, 30 PTO**

allowed tread-width adjustment from 48 to 80 inches, while the round-tube design adjusted from 68 to 88 inches.

The 420 Tricycle tractor and its 28-inch rear wheels gave 21 inches of crop clearance. The standard equipment included a three-point hitch and Dual Touch-O-Matic.

Phase one serial numbers are 80001 to 94750; phase two, 100022 to 119764; and phase three, 125003 to 136864. All-fuel production totaled 234 units, and the 420 Tricycle was the leader in LP gas vehicles, with 225 copies made.

The 420 Tricycle weighed 2,850 pounds, and was listed at $2,090.

Model 420 Utility: 1956–1958

"The Handy, Economical, Low-Built 2-3 Plow Tractor for Field, Orchard, Grove, and Vineyard Work," is the way company advertising described the 420 Utility tractor. With a no-extra-cost optional coat of yellow paint, it could also masquerade as an industrial tractor, and as a result was found on many construction sites and maintaining road right-of-ways.

When production ceased, 4,932 Model 420U tractors had made the journey down the Dubuque assembly line. Only six of those were LP gas units, while 54 were fitted with the all-fuel engine.

This tractor had the distinction of being the only phase one model to offer power steering as an option. If the customer didn't need, or want, the standard three-point hitch, he could order his tractor without it. A wide-adjustable front axle was standard, but with only 11 to 14-1/2 inches of crop clearance, it wasn't primarily designed as a row-crop tractor.

Headlights were considered essential on automobiles almost from day one, so it seems odd that as late as 1959, lights were still considered an option on this Model 430. This option set the customer back $29.75.

Hi-Crop and Special models required considerable modification to the three-point hitch system. This view of a 1958 Model 430 Hi-Crop shows how it was done.

The weight and price were within a few pounds and bucks of its wheeled siblings.

Serial numbers 80027 and 94794 are the first and last of the phase one Utility models. Phase two first and last serial numbers are 100027 and 119709; the first and last serial numbers for the phase three tractors are 125004 and 136867.

Model 420 Standard: 1956–1958

Considered a one-row tractor with 2-3 plow power, the Standard version of the Model 420 added yet another dimension to the 420 Series. The total production of the Standard model reached 3,908 during its lifetime, with 69 of those outfitted with the all-fuel engine, and 23 fitted for LP gas fuel.

Although Dual Touch-O-Matic wasn't regular equipment on the 420 Standard, it was offered as an option.

The serial numbers for phase one tractors are 80032 to 94727; phase two, 100029 to 119710; and phase three, 125025 to 136866.

The Standard 420 was priced at $1,976 and weighed approximately 2,750 pounds.

Nebraska Test 600: Model 420 Standard
Date: 1956 Fuel: Tractor Fuel HP: 21 Drawbar, 22 Belt

Here's a bird's-eye view of a 1959 Model 430 Row-Crop Special with three obvious options: a Float-Ride seat, lights, and PTO belt pulley. The seat was about $50, lights about $30, and the belt pulley about $70.

Model 420 Hi-Crop: 1956–1958

The crop clearance underneath this tractor measured a full 32 inches, which made it ideal for bedded crops. It proved to be one of the most popular Hi-Crop tractors John Deere ever manufactured, with 610 vehicles produced. All were gasoline burners, with the exception of 47 all-fuel tractors and four LP gas vehicles.

To add longitudinal stability, the 420 Hi-Crop added a 7-inch approximate spacer in front of the transmission, a feature that was introduced on the Model 40 Hi-Crop. The three-point hitch was an option, while Dual Touch-O-Matic was standard equipment.

The Hi-Crop never received the slant steering wheel during phase three production, and the directional reverser and power-adjust rear wheels were not available.

The Hi-Crop weighed approximately 3,450 pounds and carried a price tag of $2,328 for a base model.

The serial numbers for phase one are 80231 to 94799; phase two, 100515 to 119789; and phase three, 125132 to 136856. Indications are that at least two of the phase two units were scrapped.

Model 420 Special Utility: 1957–1958

Based on the Row-Crop Utility, the Special Utility was fitted with a stronger, fixed-tread front axle and heavy-duty steering arms to take the daily punishment of front-end loaders at commercial job sites. To assist the operator in this situation, it offered power-assisted steering as an option.

The Model 420 Special Utility wasn't produced until April 1957, thus there was no phase one production. Only 255 copies were produced during phases two and three, all of which were gasoline fuel models.

This unit weighed approximately 3,200 pounds and was priced at $2,210 as a no-frills basic tractor.

The serial numbers for phase two tractors are 114632 to 119576; phase three, 125001 to 130578.

Model 420 Special: 1956–1958

Sometimes called the Semi Hi-Crop or Southern Special, this high-clearance version provided 26 inches of under-the-axle clearance. It didn't have the spacer in front of the transmission, as did the true Hi-Crop, and it used 34-inch rear tires and a shorter adjustable front axle. Like the Hi-Crop, it retained the straight-vertical steering wheel throughout its production. Standard equipment included three-point hitch and dual Touch-O-Matic.

The Special had the lowest total production numbers of any Model 420 version, with only 86 copies produced. All were gas burners, with the exception of three all-fuel tractors. It weighed about the same 3,100 pounds as the Tricycle model, but was a little more pricey at $2,195.

The serial numbers for phase one are 80091 to 94363; phase two, 100330 to 119064; and phase three, 125309 to 135242.

Model 430 Series: 1958–1960

Operator comfort and convenience were the focus of engineers when the 20 Series tractors were upgraded to the 30 Series. The two-cylinder engines were the same as featured in the 20 Series tractors and produced the same horsepower ratings, although no 430 model tractors were tested at Nebraska. For specs on the 30 Series tractors, see the information on the corresponding Model 420 tractors.

All Model 430 tractors were available in three fuel options: gasoline, all-fuel, and LP gas.

All 430 vehicles, regardless of which model, received sequentially numbered serial numbers, beginning with 140001 and ending with 161096.

Model 430 Standard: 1958–1960

Anyone seeking a low-production 30 Series tractor should consider the LP gas 430 Standard, as only five were produced,

Continues on page 126

MASSEY-FERGUSON TO-35 DIESEL: 1958-1961

As the demand for power escalated, Massey-Ferguson (MF) put more horses under the hood on all tractors. The result was a muscled-up Ferguson line, seemingly at the cost of the small utility tractor. The "little Fergie" was bulked up, and now the upgraded TO 35 Diesel was the baby of the Ferguson family.

In appearance, it still bore a strong resemblance to the Ford-Ferguson family that had grown out of the 9N design. Diesel power was gaining in popularity, especially overseas, and MF was to become one of the leaders in diesel power. To that end, in 1959, it purchased the F. Perkins Ltd. company of Peterborough, England, giving the manufacturer a wide selection of proven diesel engines to use in tractor production.

The initial version of the MF TO 35 Diesel came fitted with a four-cylinder Standard Motor 23-C vertical engine with a 3-5/16x4-inch bore and stroke. It was rated at 2,000 rpm and displaced 137.8-ci. After MF purchased the Perkins plant, almost all MF tractors were fitted with a Perkins powerplant. In the case of the MF 35 Diesel, it was the Perkins 3A-152 three-cylinder vertical I-head with a 3-5/8x5-inch bore and stroke that upped the displacement to 152.7-ci. The change to the Perkins diesel engine kicked the MF 35 into the three-plow tractor ranks. Regardless of the engine, the tractor sported a 6/2 transmission with forward speeds from 1.33 to 14.57 miles per hour.

Industrial and Vineyard versions of the TO 35 Diesel were also produced. The Vineyard model had a minimum tread width of 32 inches, with an overall width of 46 inches. The tractor weight, with either engine, fell at approximately 3,200 pounds without weights or ballast.

Customers could expect to pay about $3,000 to $3,330 to purchase a TO 35.

Nebraska Test 690: Massey-Ferguson TO 35 Diesel
Date: 1959 Fuel: Diesel   HP: 30 Drawbar, 32 PTO
Nebraska Test 744: Massey-Ferguson TO 35 Diesel
Date: 1960 Fuel: Diesel   HP: 33 Drawbar, 37 PTO

This is a fine example of a 1959 Model 435 Diesel, the last two-cylinder tractor introduced by Deere & Company. The total production for the 435 was 4,626 copies.

This restored crawler, a 1959 Model 430C, has the five-roller track, directional reverser, and three-point hitch.

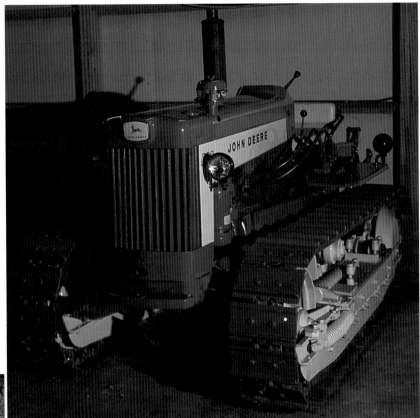

This Model 430 Hi-Crop just begs to be photographed, so here's another view.

ALLIS-CHALMERS D-10 AND D-12: 1959-1968

The smallest of Allis-Chalmers' (AC) new line of D Series tractors were the D-10 and D-12, which started rolling down the assembly lines in May 1959 as replacements for the Model B and Model CA. Both vehicles underwent several upgrades and changes during their lifetime, but information given here will reflect the specifications as they were introduced in 1959.

The only real difference between the Model D-10 and Model D-12 was the tread width; otherwise the specs were identical. The tread width on the D-10 ranged from 42 to 72 inches, while on the D-12 it was 52 to 79-1/4 inches.

Considered marginal two-plow tractors or one- and two-row row-crop vehicles, they were powered by an AC-built four-cylinder vertical engine. The bore and stroke measured 3 3/8x3 7/8-inch and provided 138.7-ci. The gasoline burner was rated at 1,650 rpm. A basic 4/1 tranny gave working speeds of 2, 3-1/2, and 4-1/2 miles per hour, while road gear hustled along at 11-1/2 miles per hour.

Dual and single front-wheel tricycle models were dropping in popularity across the board, so AC only offered the D-10 and D-12 in wide-adjustable front axle. The only other version of these two tractors was the high-clearance model, which provided 4 additional inches of crop clearance.

In 1959, the American Society of Agricultural Engineers (ASAE) made it official that in the final analysis, Harry Ferguson had won. In 1917, Ferguson began his quest for a better plow design, which led to the Ford-Ferguson 9N tractor, which featured his three-point hitch and hydraulic system. During the following two decades, tractor engineers designed the Quik-Tatch, the Fast Hitch, the Snap-Coupler, and the Eagle Hitch, all in an effort to develop a superior mounted hitch system.

However, in 1959 the ASAE, along with the Farm and Industrial Equipment Institute (FIEI) and the SAE, adopted a proposal that made the three-point system for hitching implements to agricultural wheel tractors the standard throughout the industry. Allis-Chalmers responded by continuing to offer its Snap-Coupler system plus a bare-bones lift-lower three-point system.

The D-12 and D-10 tractors weighed in at about 2,860 pounds. The D-10 listed at $2,610, the D-12 at $2,760. Approximately 5,304 copies of the D-10 and 4,070 copies of the D-12 were produced at the company's West Allis, Wisconsin, production facilities.

Nebraska Test 723: Allis-Chalmers D-12
Date: 1959 Fuel: Gasoline   HP: 24 Drawbar, 28 Belt
Nebraska Test 724: Allis-Chalmers D-10
Date: 1959 Fuel: Gasoline   HP: 25 Drawbar, 28 PTO

Continued from page 122

or the all-fuel version, of which 18 were manufactured. Gasoline copies of the 430 Standard tallied a total 1,786.

The looks were all that varied between the Model 420 Standard and the 430 Standard, of which 1,809 were produced. The 430 Standard carried a price tag of $2,118.50.

Model 430 Utility: 1958–1960

A total of 1,340 copies of this ground-hugging model exited the Dubuque assembly plant. Three of these were LP gas models, and 10 were all-fuel versions.

About $1,847.25 could make an individual the proud owner of a no-frills Model 430 Utility.

Model 430 Row-Crop Utility: 1958–1960

Almost twice as many 430 Row-Crop Utilities were built as any other single version of the Model 420 tractors, with a total of 5,981 copies rolling off the production line. There were 68 LP gas and 88 all-fuel vehicles manufactured.

It was the third-most-expensive wheeled version, at $2,350 for the base model.

Model 430 Tricycle: 1958–1960

With 3,255 copies manufactured, the Tricycle was the second most popular of the 430 models. It was also the most popular LP gas tractor of the 430s, with 128 copies produced. There were 33 all-fuel vehicles made in the Tricycle configuration.

The dual-front-wheel tricycle model listed at $1,845.50; the single-front-wheel version at $1,859.50; and the wide-adjustable front axle at $1,994.25.

Model 430 Hi-Crop: 1958–1960

The 430 Hi-Crop's dash and steering wheel now had the same styling as the rest of the line, with the exception of the five custom LP gas Hi-Crop 430s built at the Dubuque facility. These were a throwback to the Model 420 vertical steering wheel and dash.

There were only 27 all-fuel versions of this tractor produced, which makes them a desirable low-production model. There were a total of 183 gasoline vehicles produced, which brings the total number of 430 Hi-Crop tractors to 215.

The base list price was $2,497, and today the value would be right up there at the top of Model 430 tractors.

Model 430V Special: 1958–1960

The Special, Southern Special, or Semi Hi-Crop tractors, were gasoline burners, all 63 produced. This was the second-most-costly 420 wheel tractor, with a base list price of $2,360.

Model 430 Crawler: 1958–1960

As with its predecessor, the 420 Crawler, customers could specify either a four- or five-roller frame or an all-fuel engine. Customers chose the all-fuel option 33 times. Or, they could specify the LP gas powerplant, which they did only four times.

Find one of these rusting away in a hedgerow, and if you don't have a heart attack, buy it. You'll have a rare collector's piece. The gasoline units numbered 2,203, making a grand total of 2,240 copies of the 430 Crawler.

A new four-roller Crawler demanded about $3,246.75. The five-roller model listed at about $3,529.25.

Both a yellow Crawler and yellow-wheel version of the Model 430 were offered through Deere's Industrial Division.

The 430 tractors carried the same engine and drivetrain as the 420 models, so Nebraska certified that the 430 tractors had the same test results as the 420 tractors.

MODEL 435: 1959–1960

This tractor has the distinction of being the last two-cylinder John Deere model to be introduced. Some purists would argue that it shouldn't be considered a real two-cylinder John Deere, because the exhaust note sounds very different and the engine isn't a John Deere product. The engine was a General Motors vertical two-cylinder, two-cycle diesel. The supercharged engine has a 3-7/8x4-1/2-inch bore and stroke, which amounted to 106.1-ci with a rated rpm of 1,850. The standard tranny was a 4/1, with a 5/1 offered as an option. With the exception of the different engine, the Model 435 is essentially a Model 430 Row-Crop Utility with different footwear.

Deere's first small diesel weighed approximately 3,200 pounds, and in 1960 the list price was $3,190.

The serial numbers ranged from 435001 to 439626. The total production was 4,626 copies, from March 31, 1959, to February 29, 1960.

Nebraska Test 716: Model 435
Date: 1959 Fuel: Diesel HP: 28 Drawbar, 32 PTO

THE TWO-CYLINDER LEGACY

When John Deere ceased production of two-cylinder tractors, almost 1,500,000 copies had been manufactured. Now, a half-century later, these descendants of the horses and mules that they replaced are the focus of a rewarding hobby for thousands of people around the globe.

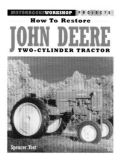

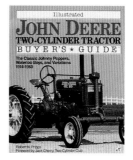

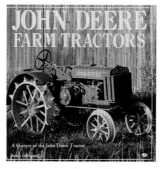

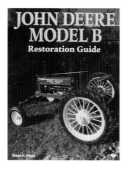
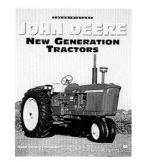
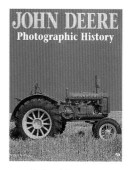